AMAZING DESIGNS

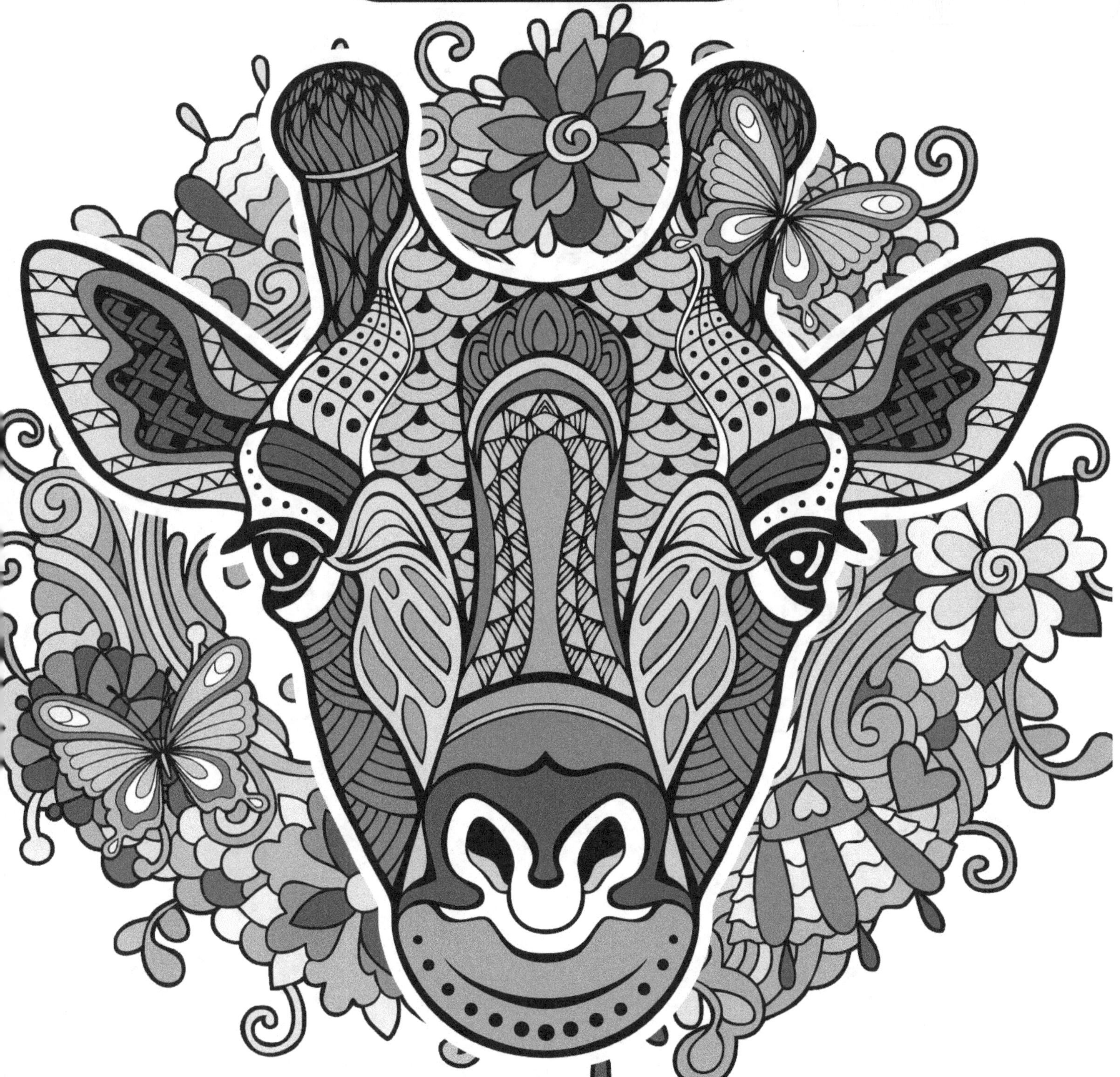

DOODLE GIRAFFES
COLORING BOOK
RELAXING PATTERNS FOR STRESS RELIEF

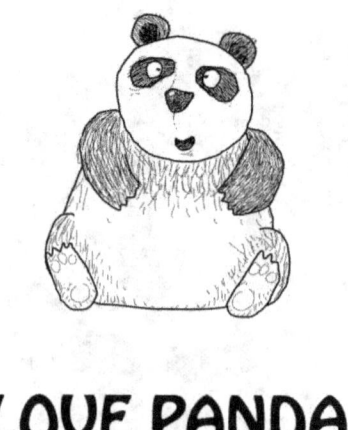

LOVE PANDA

Copyright 2017

Printed in The U.S.A.

All right reserved. This Coloring books or any potion thereof many not be reproduced or used in any manner whatsoever without the exoress written permission of the publisher except.

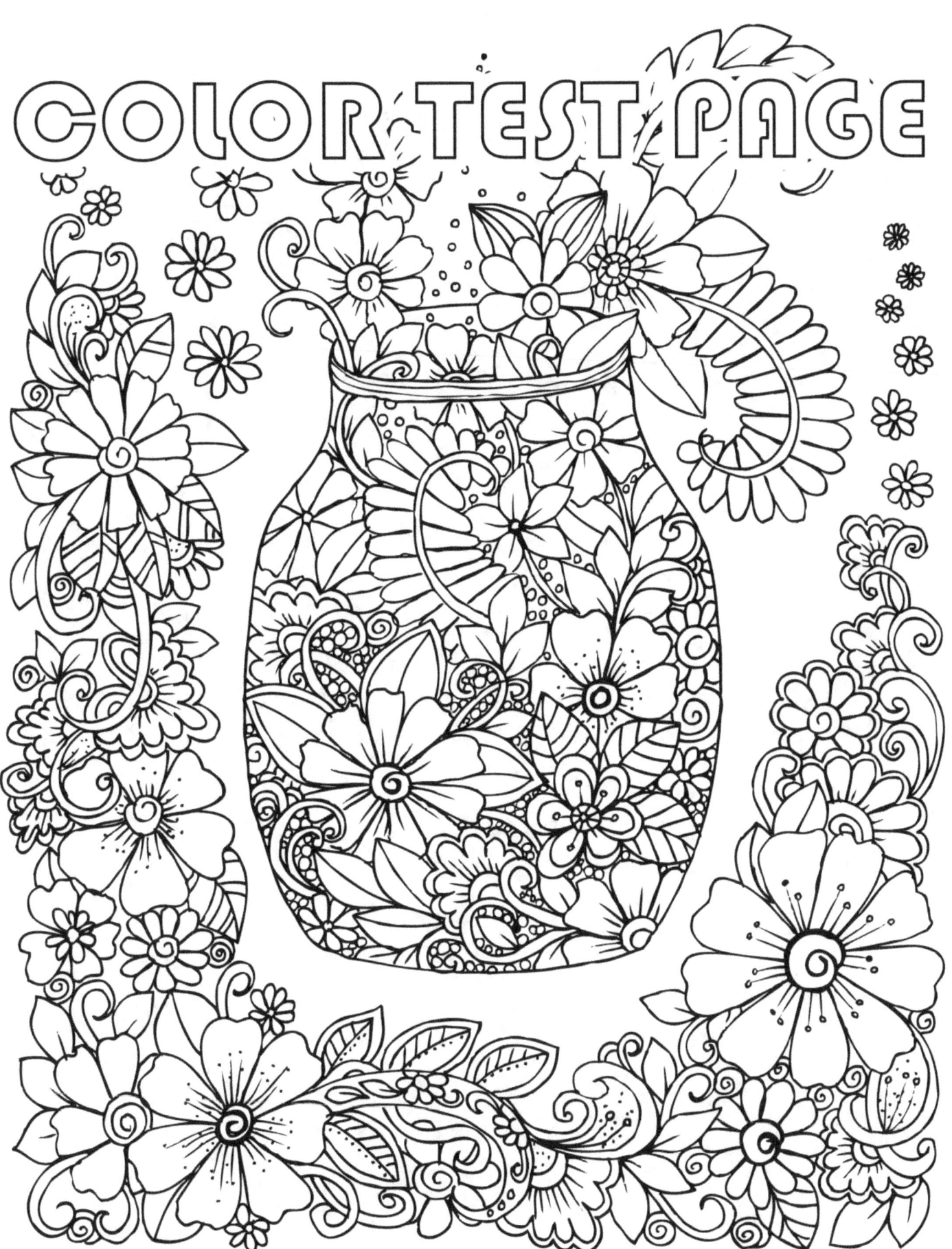

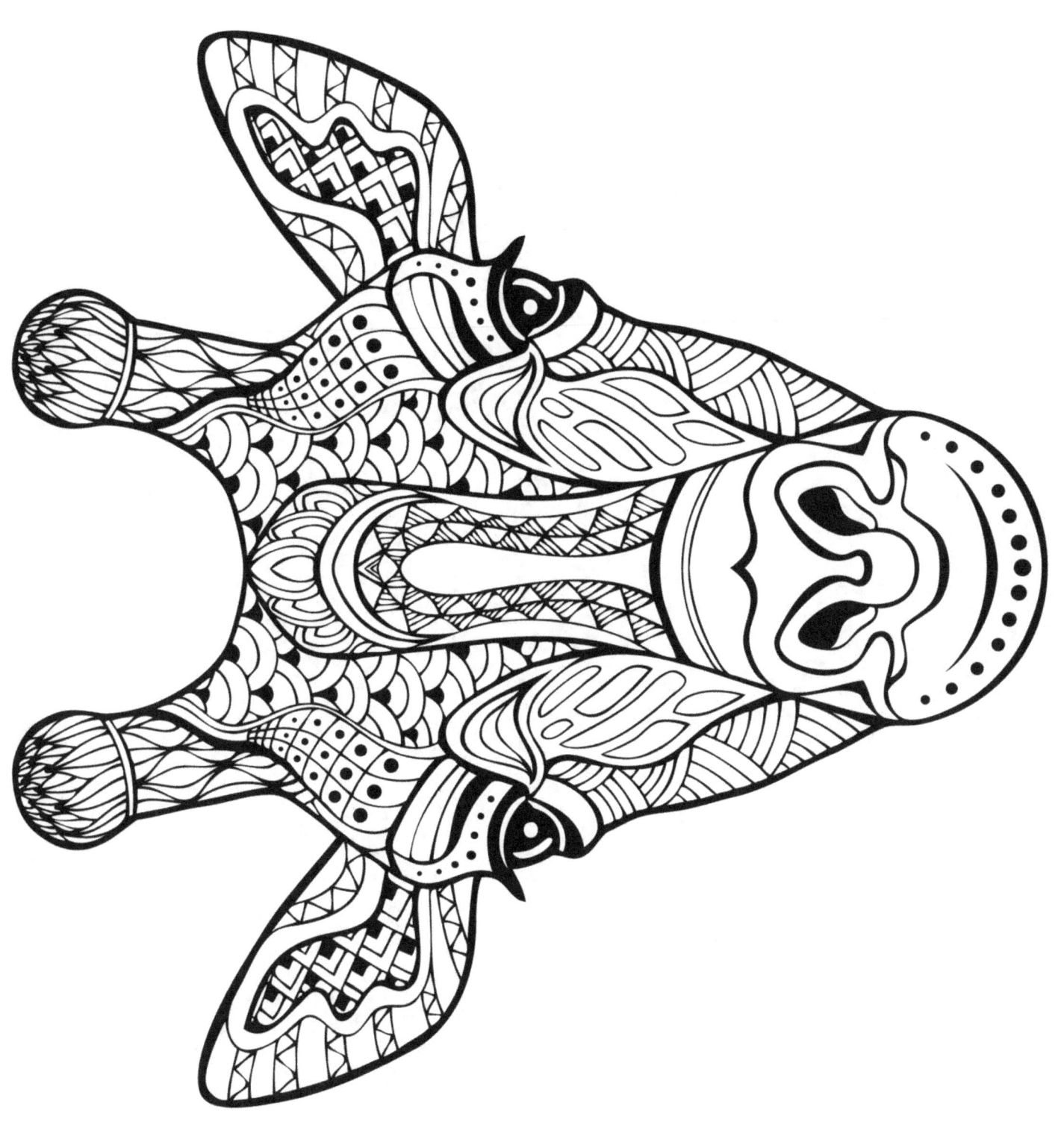

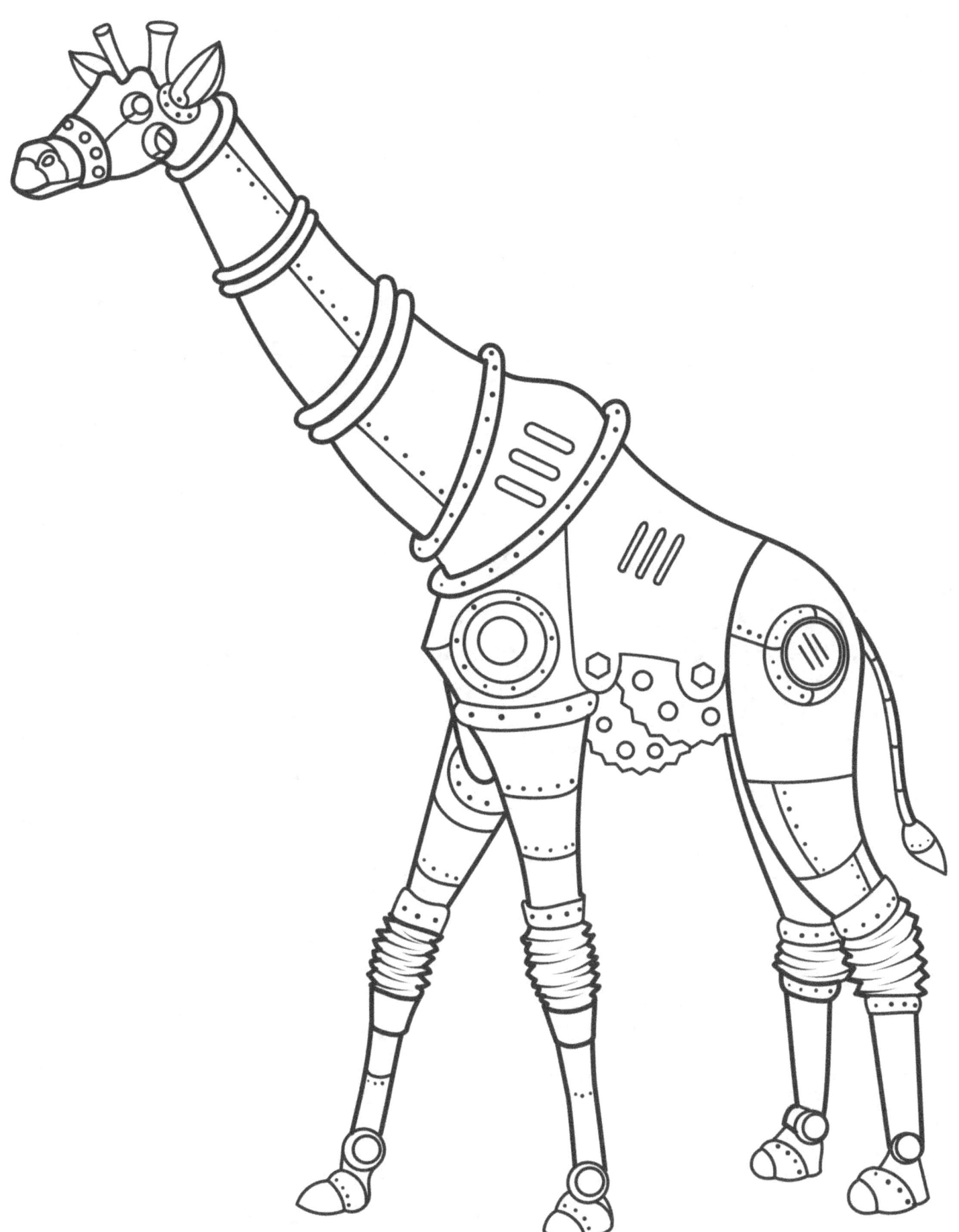

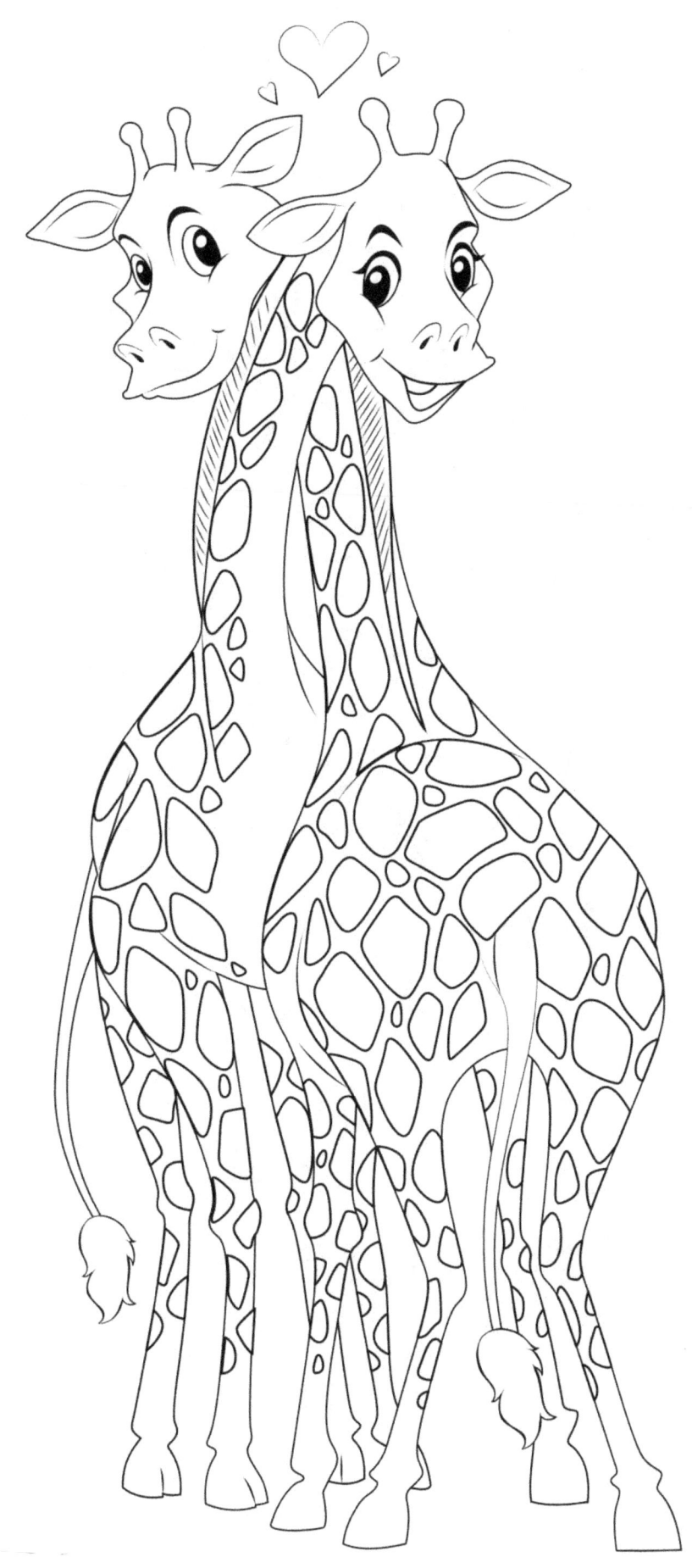

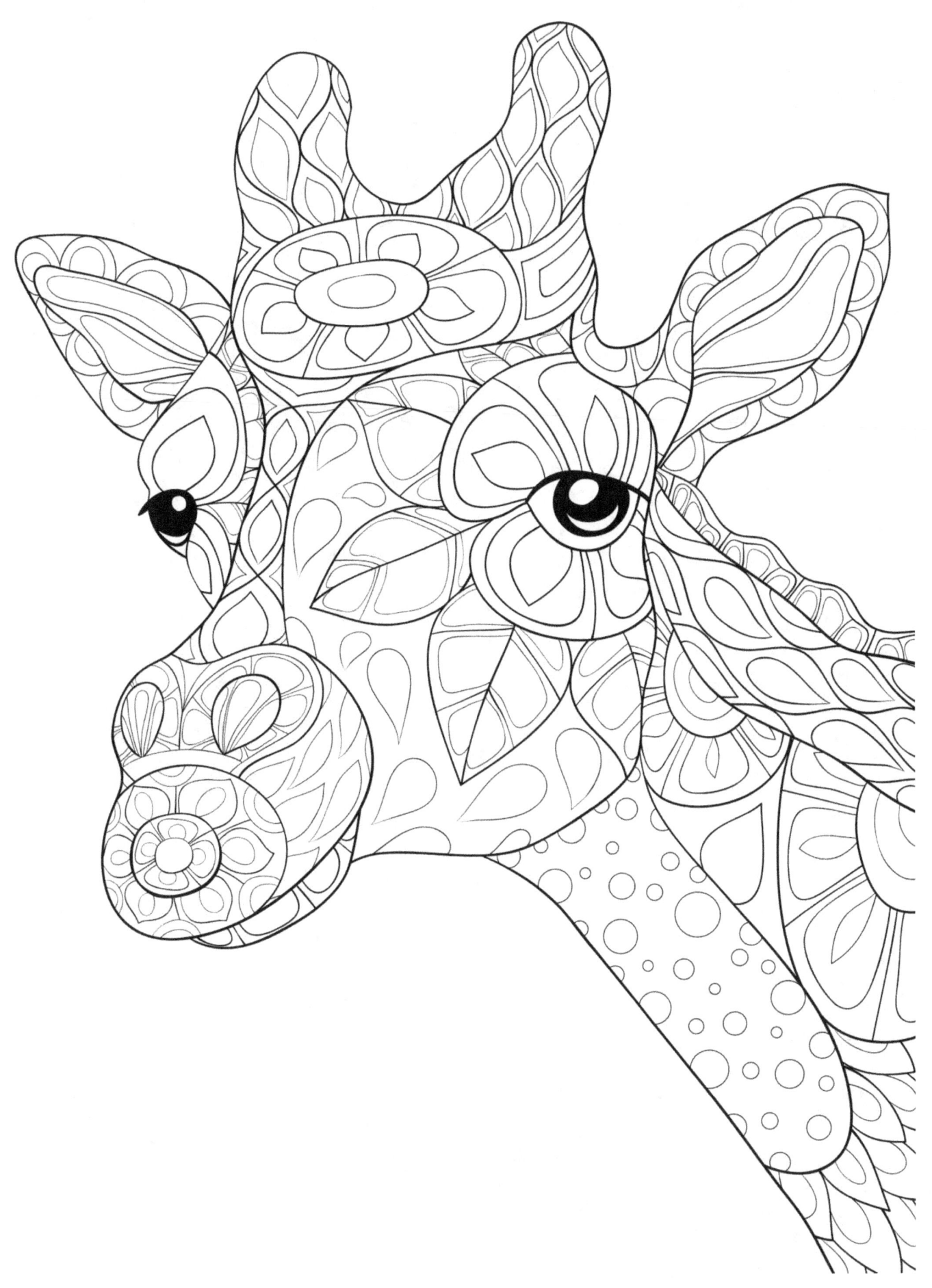

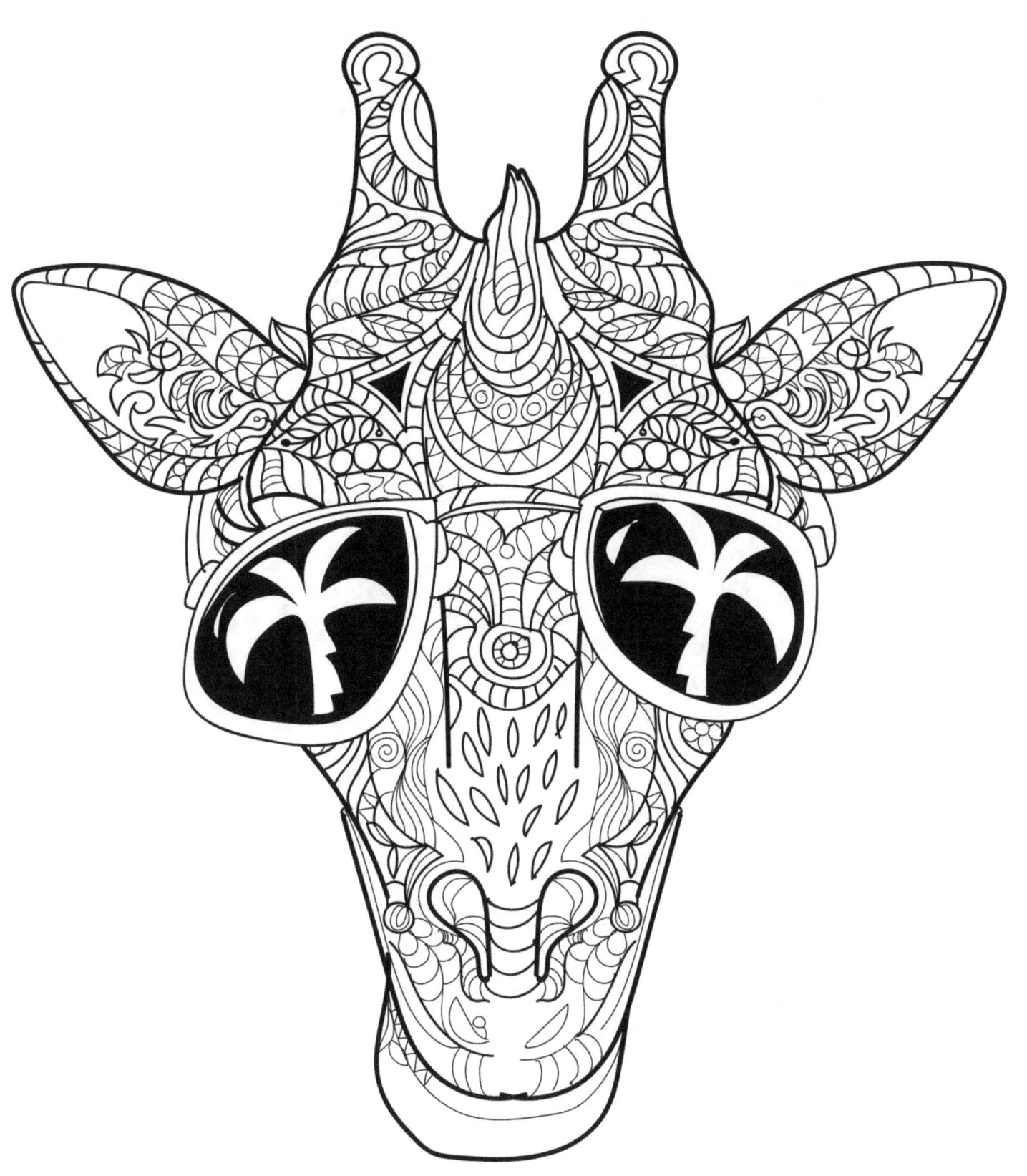

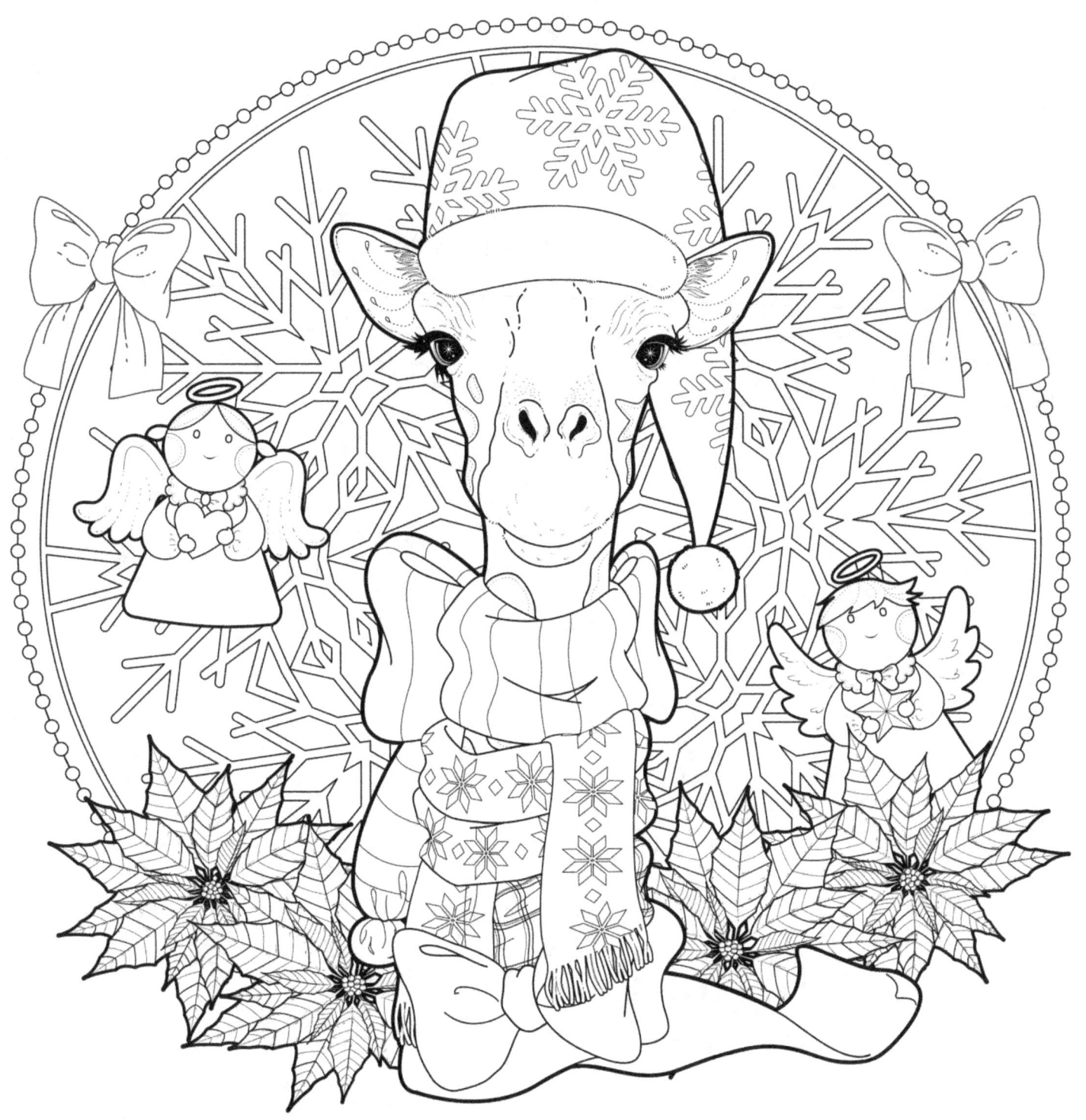

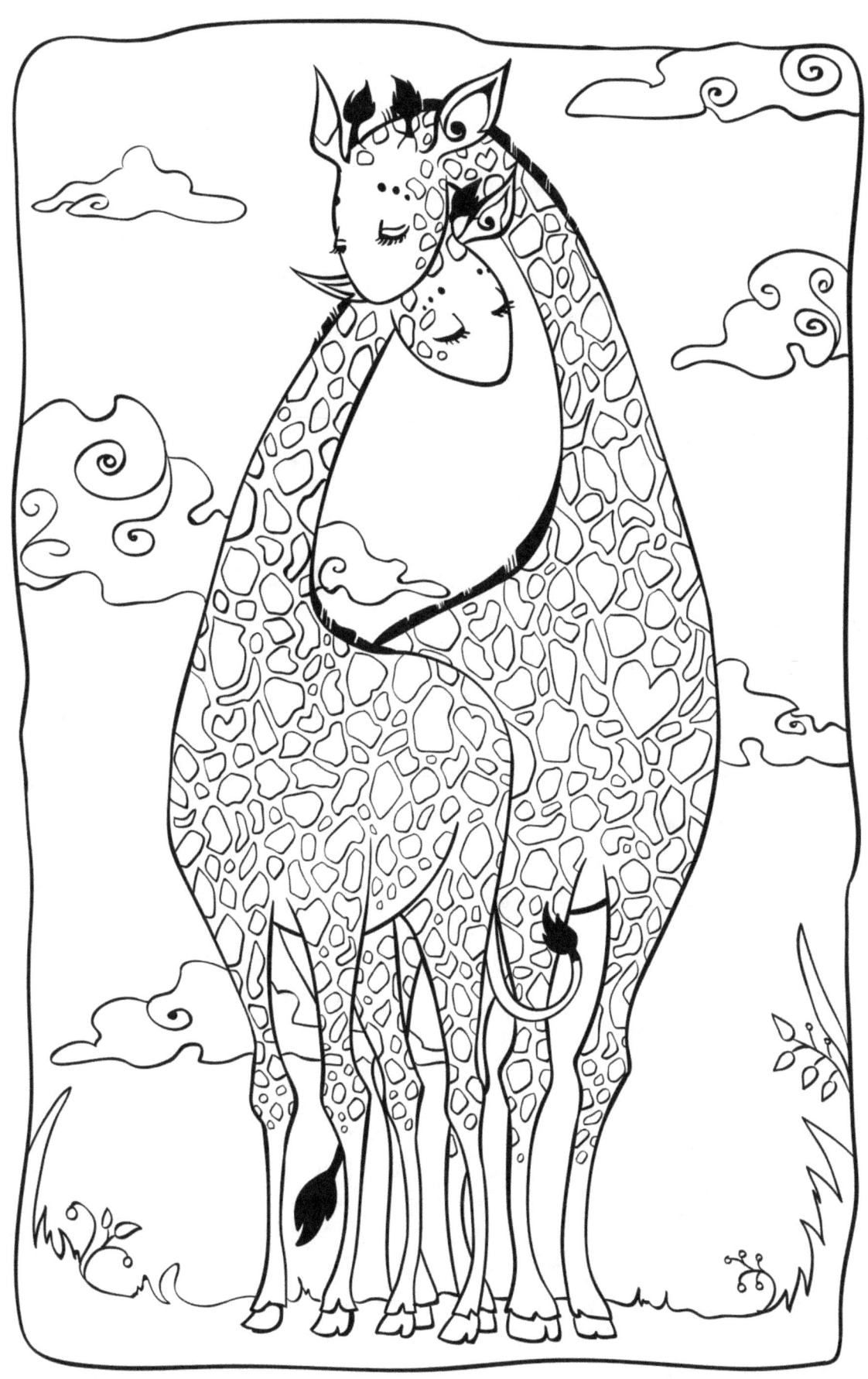

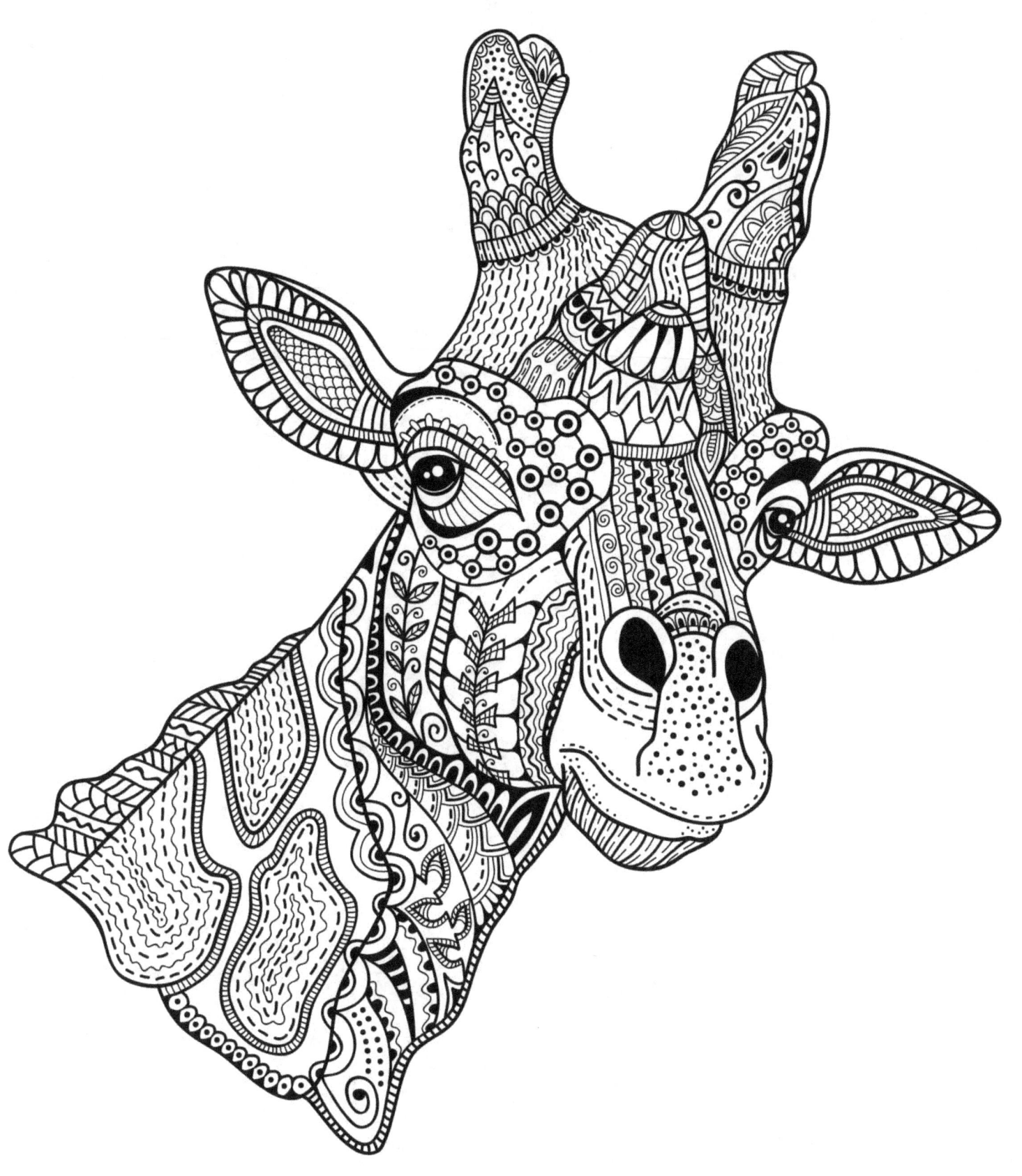

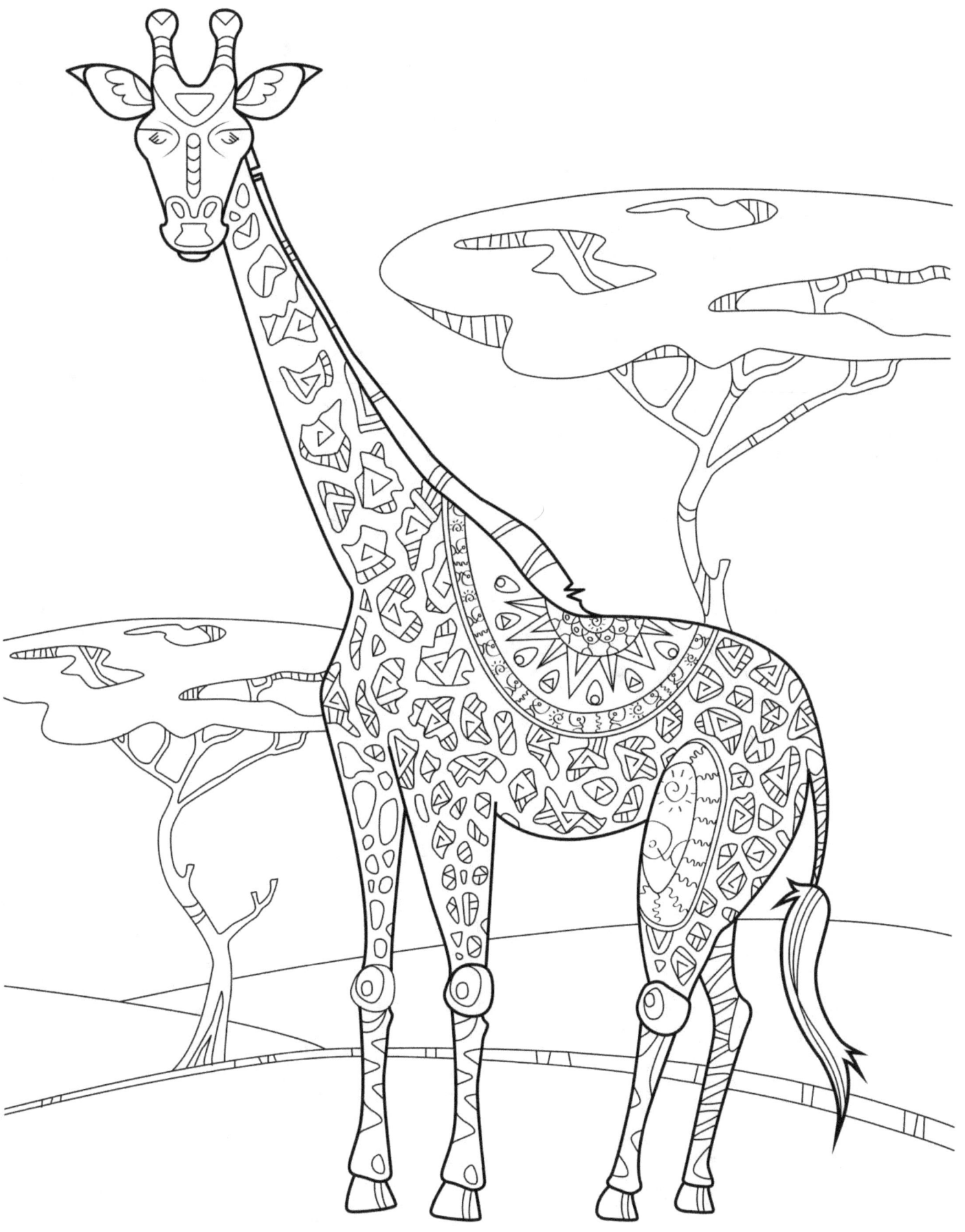

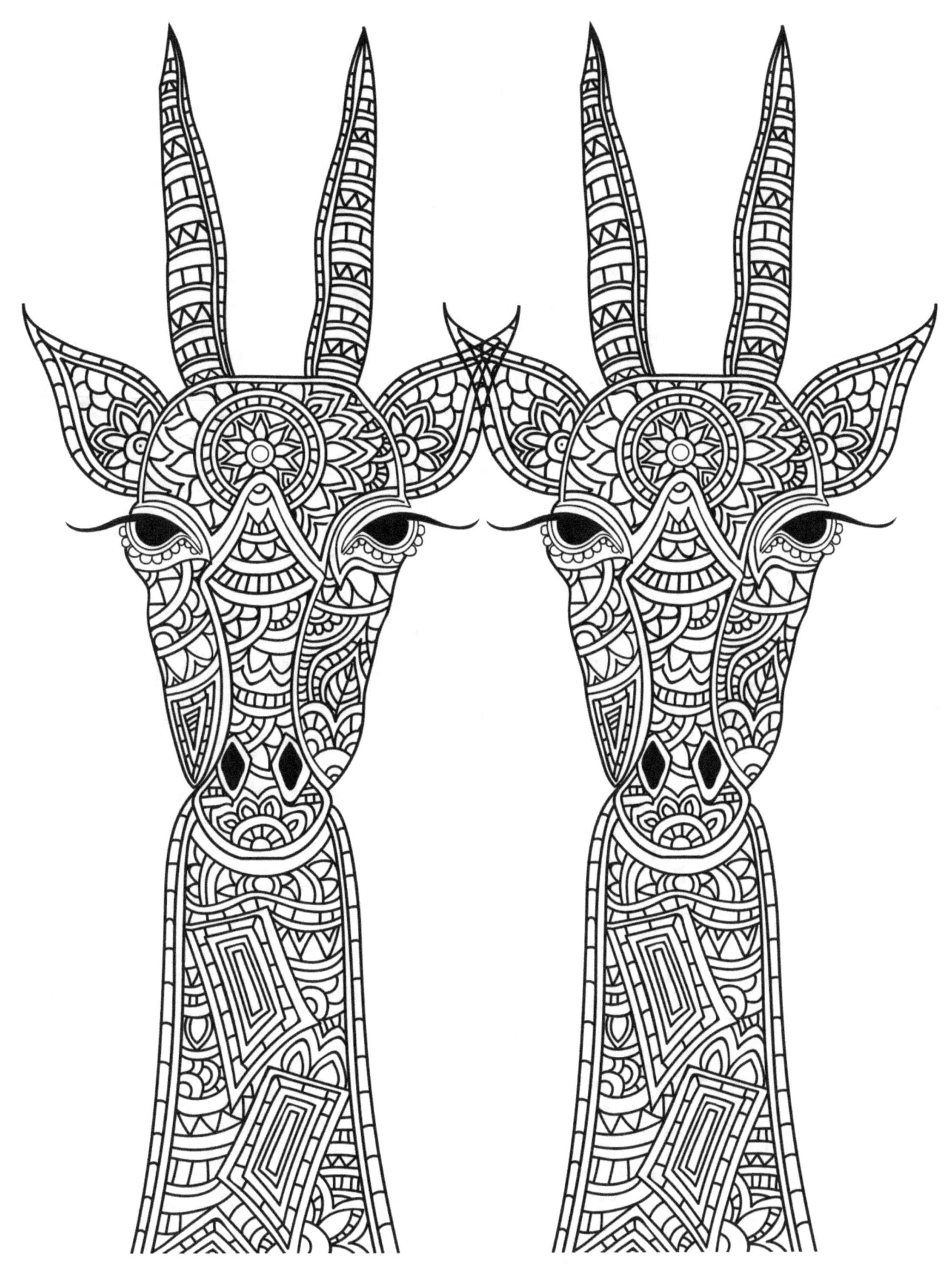

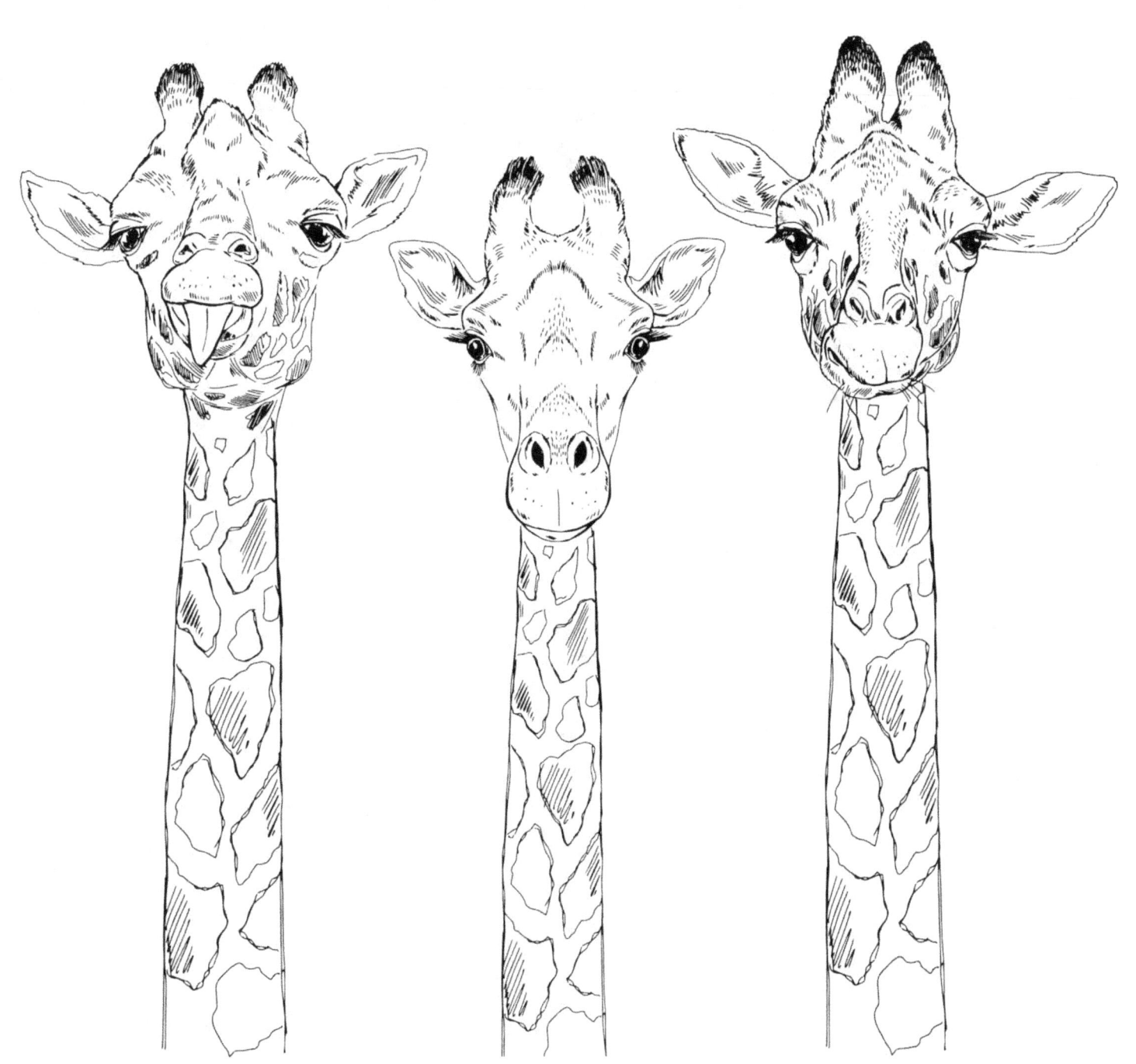

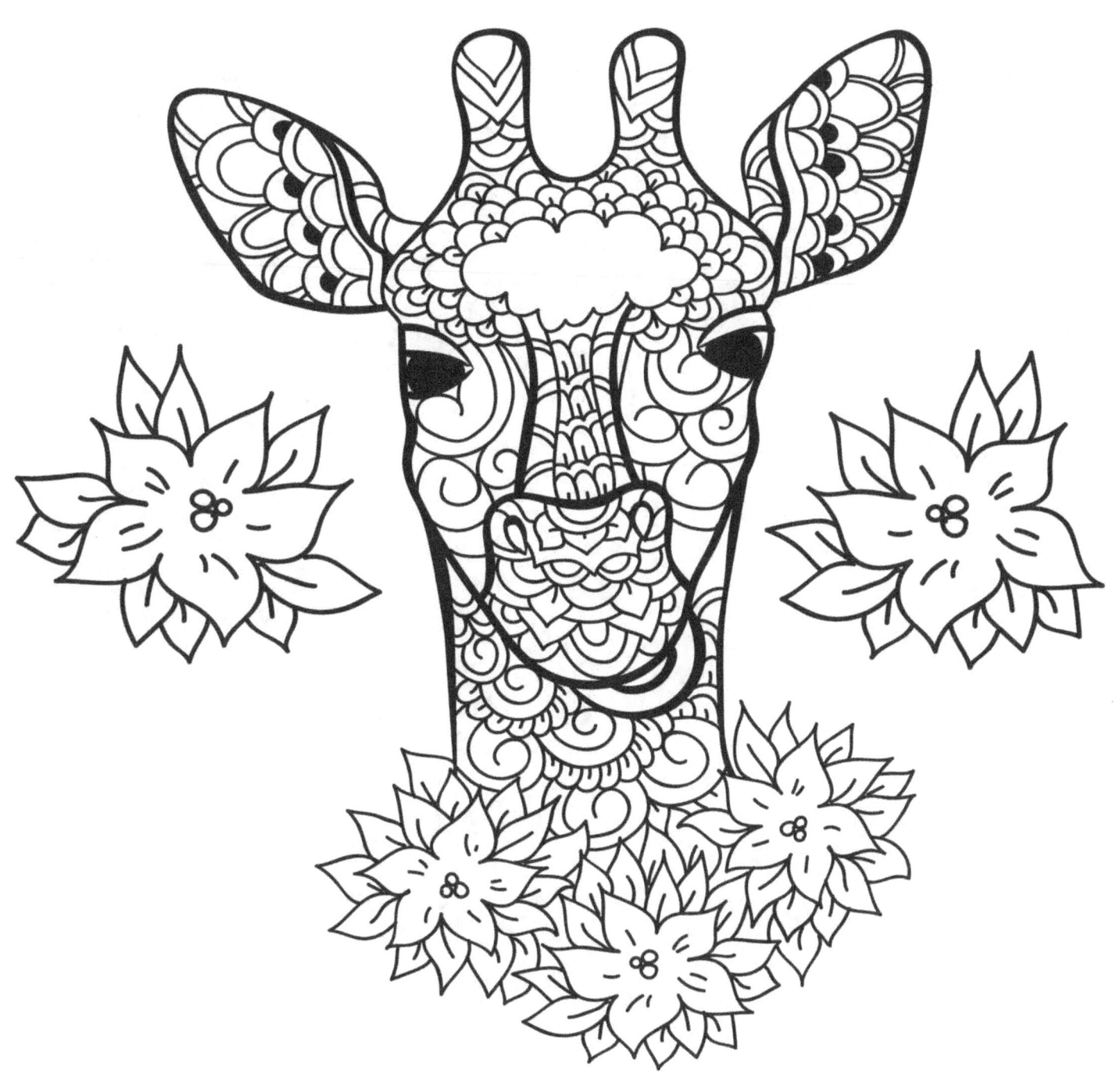

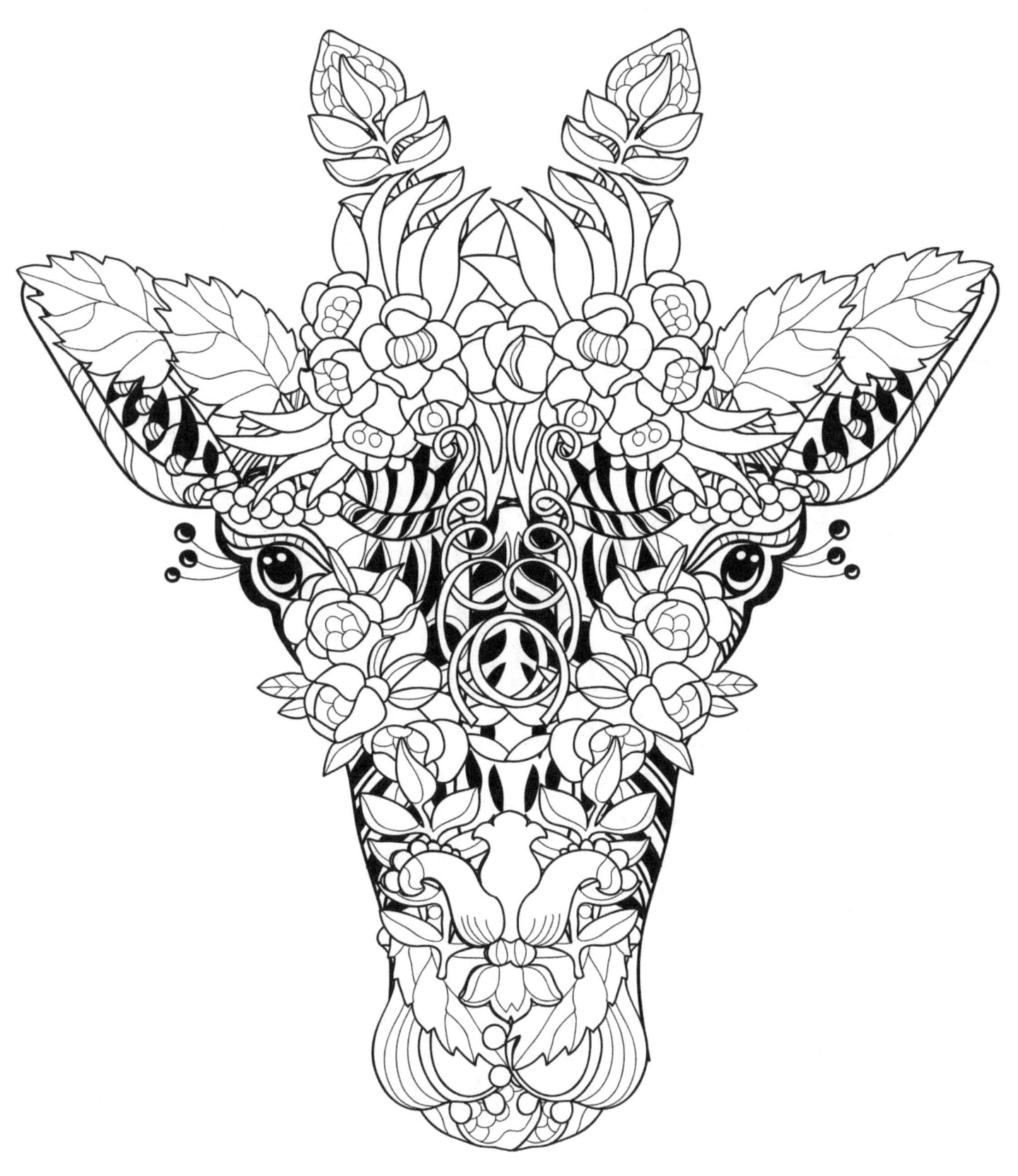

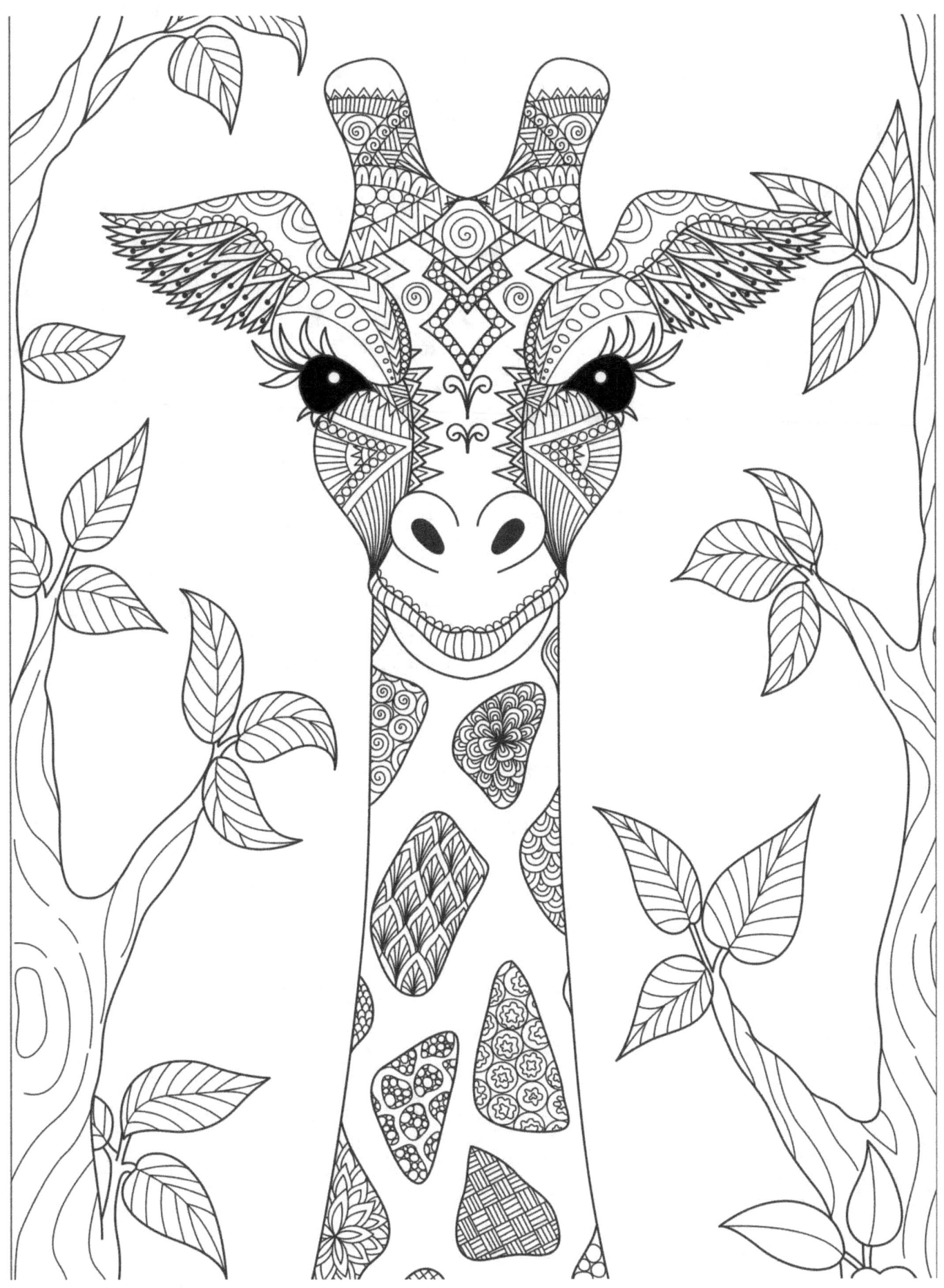

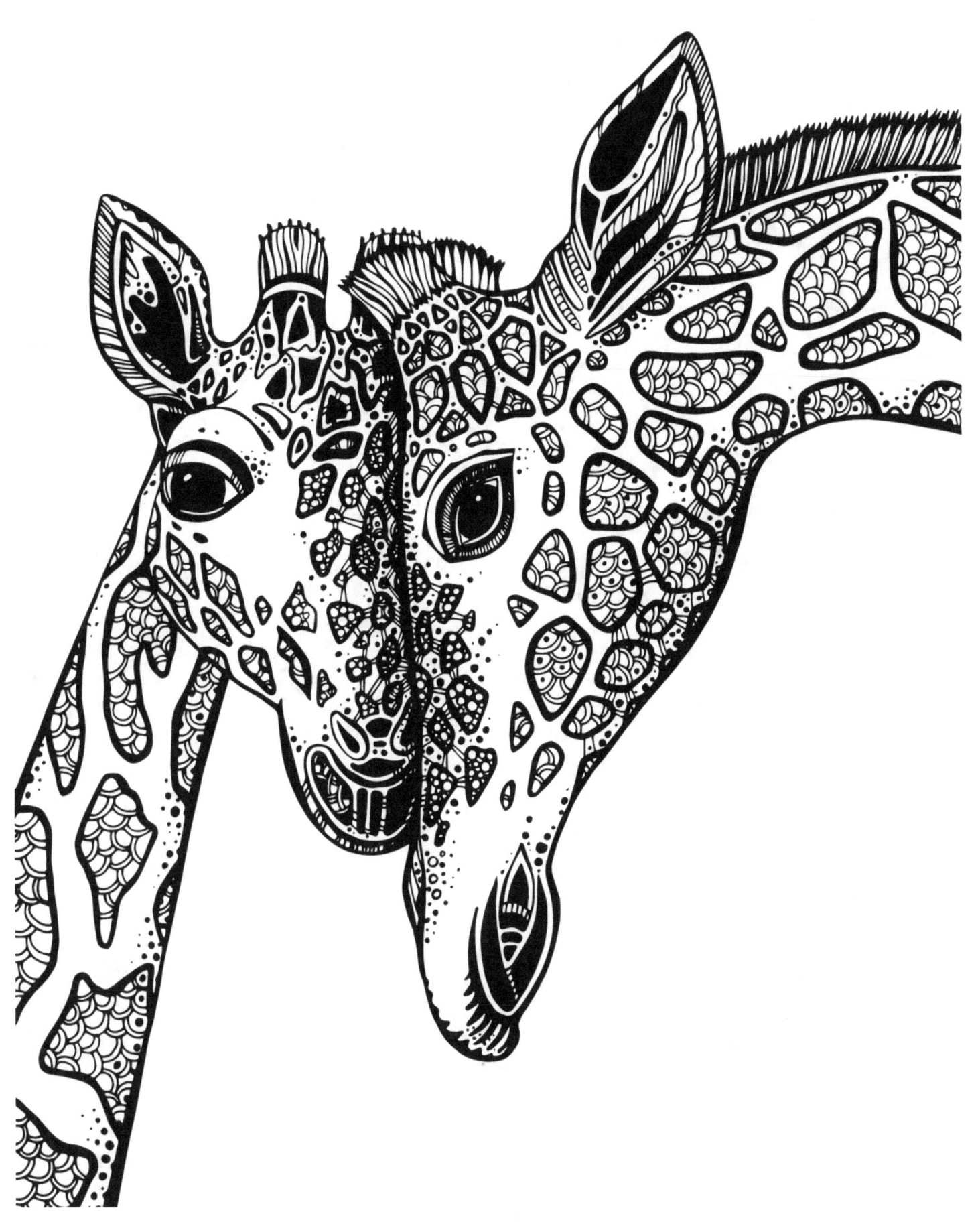

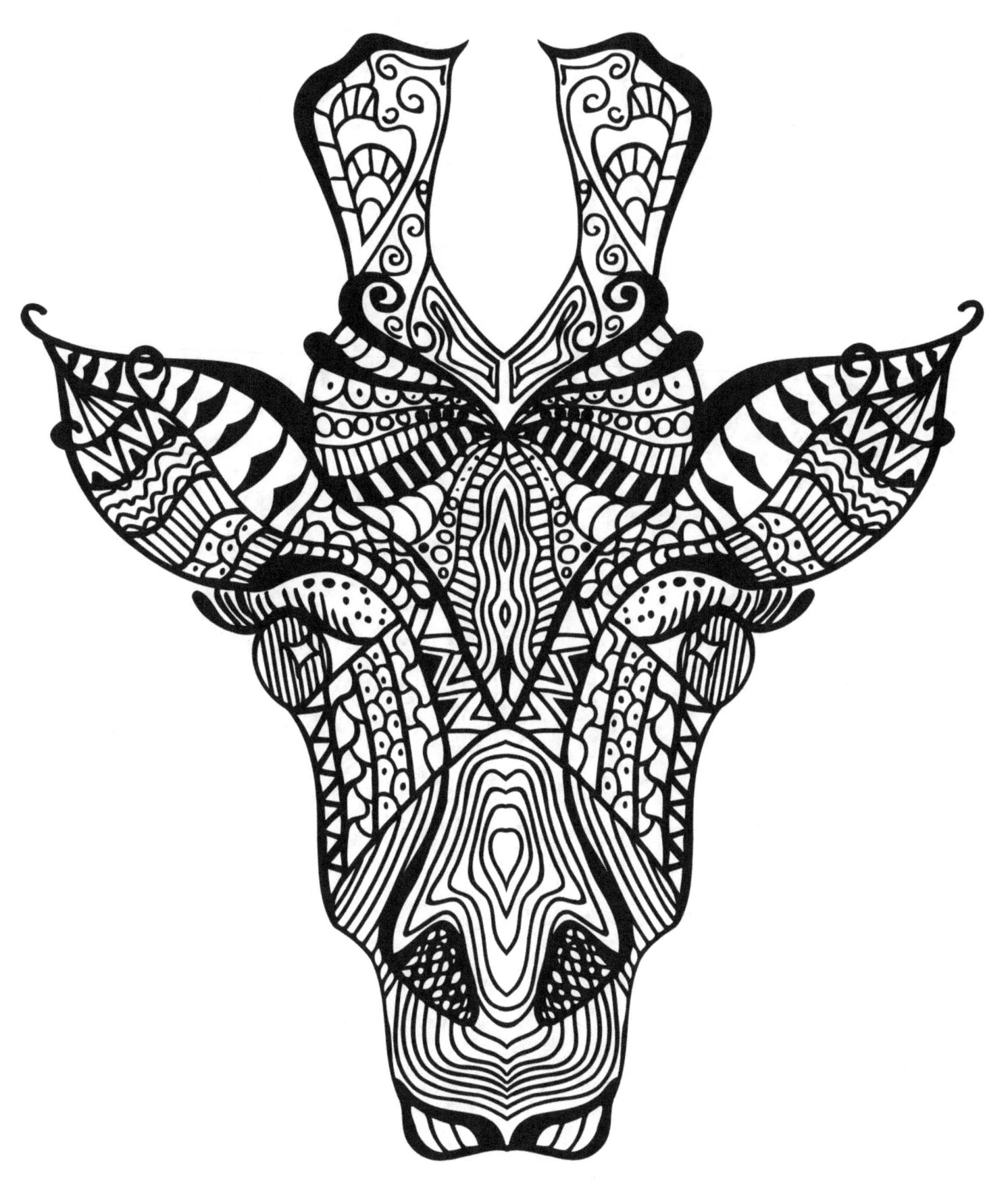

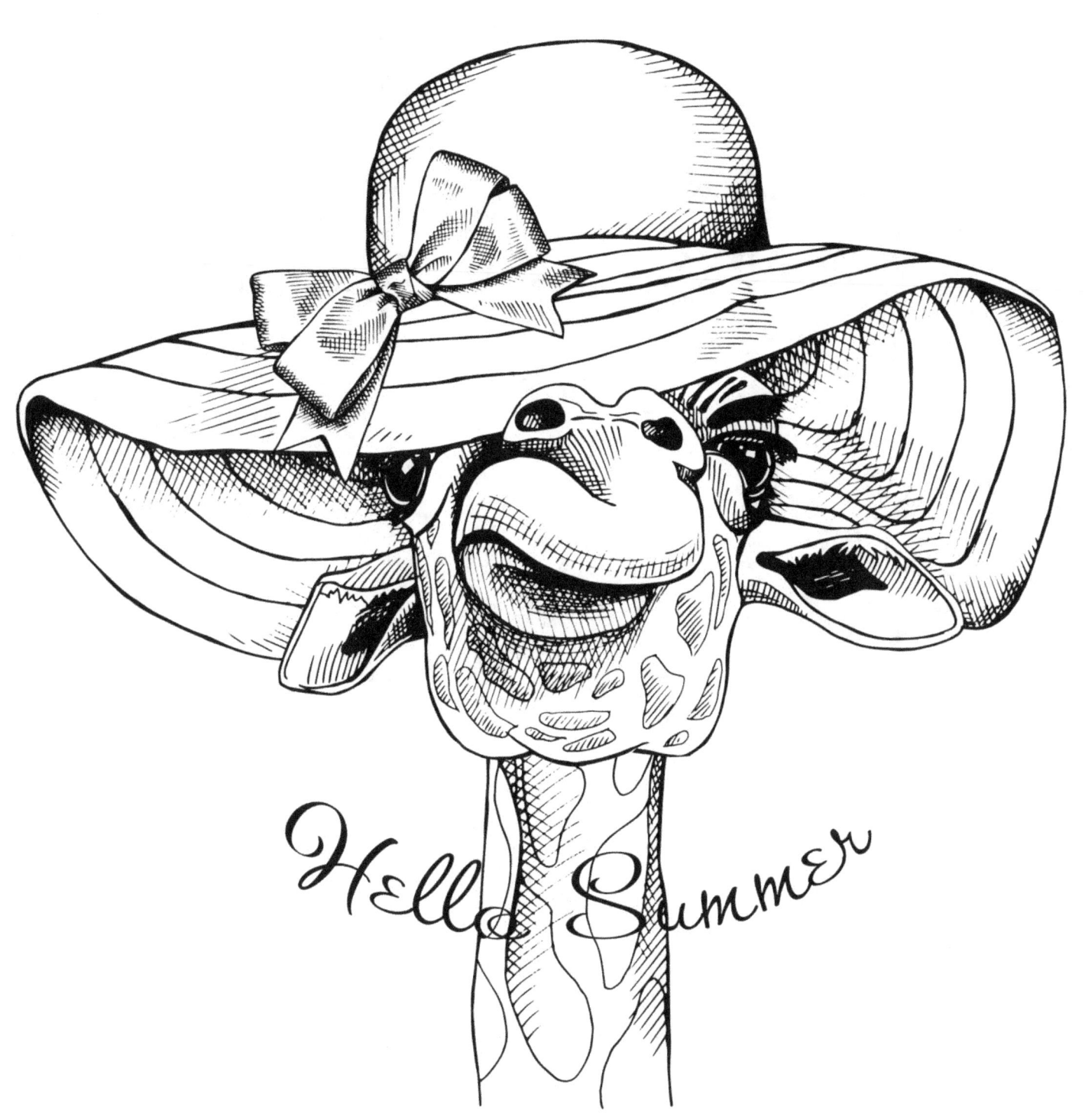

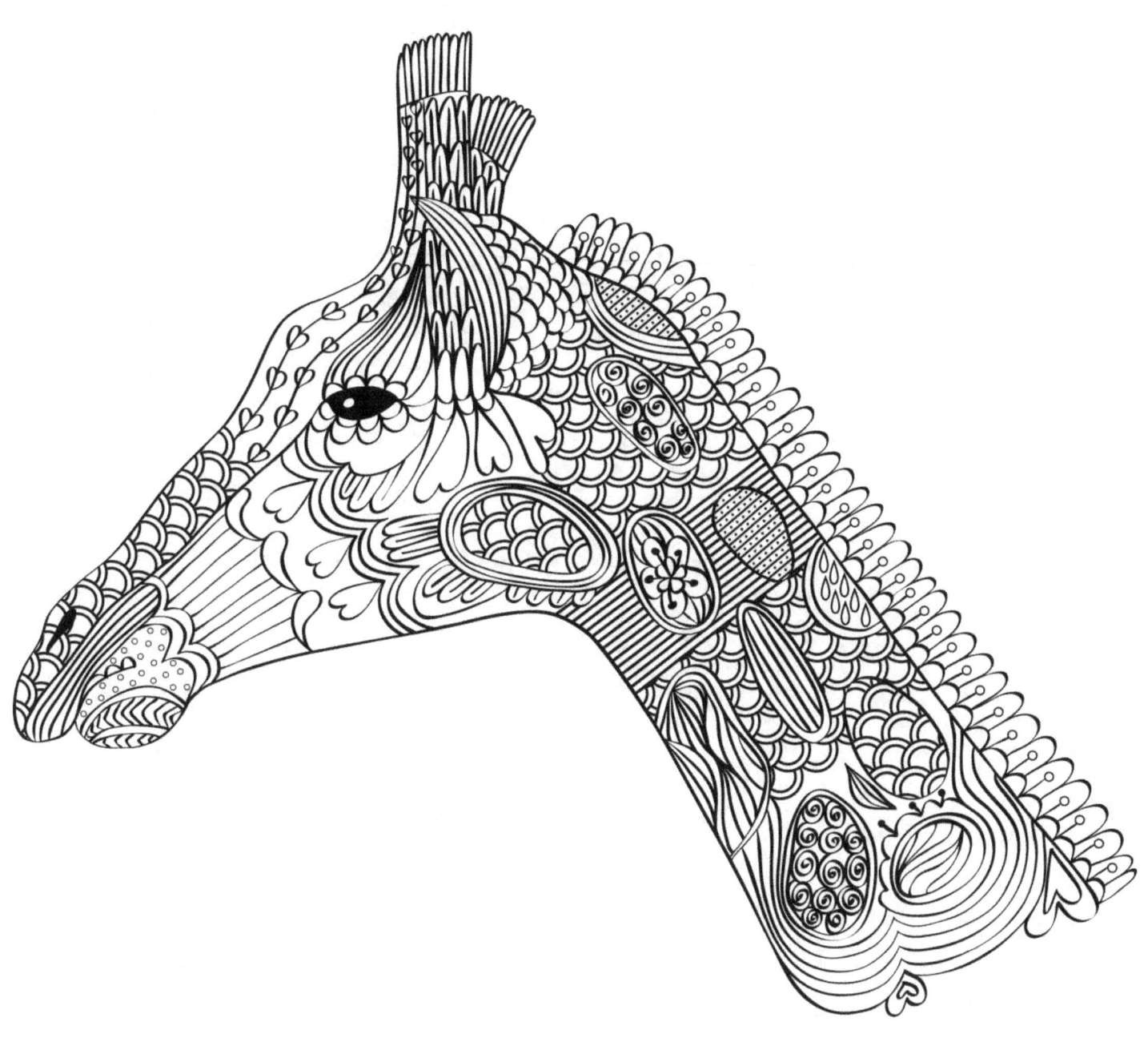

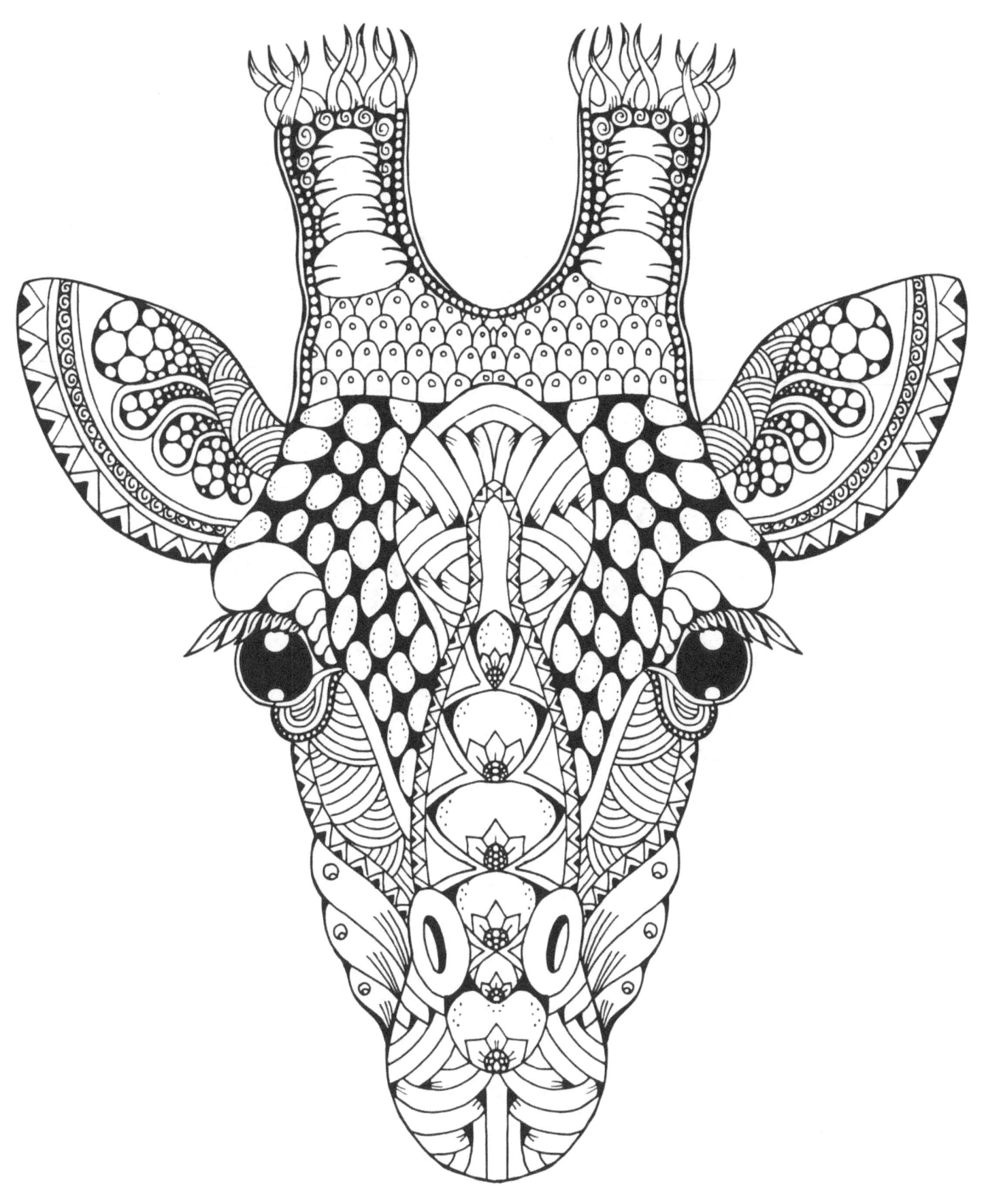

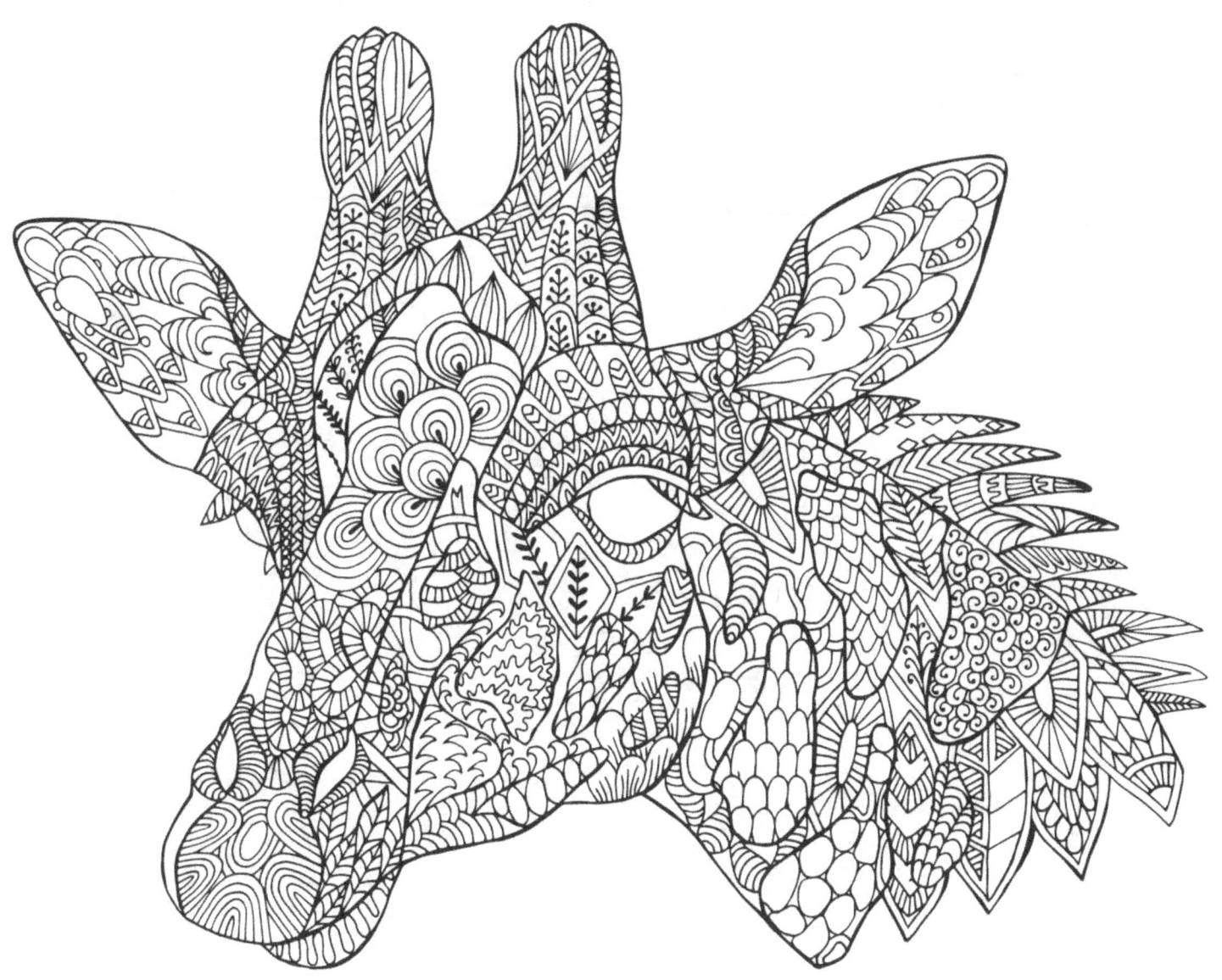

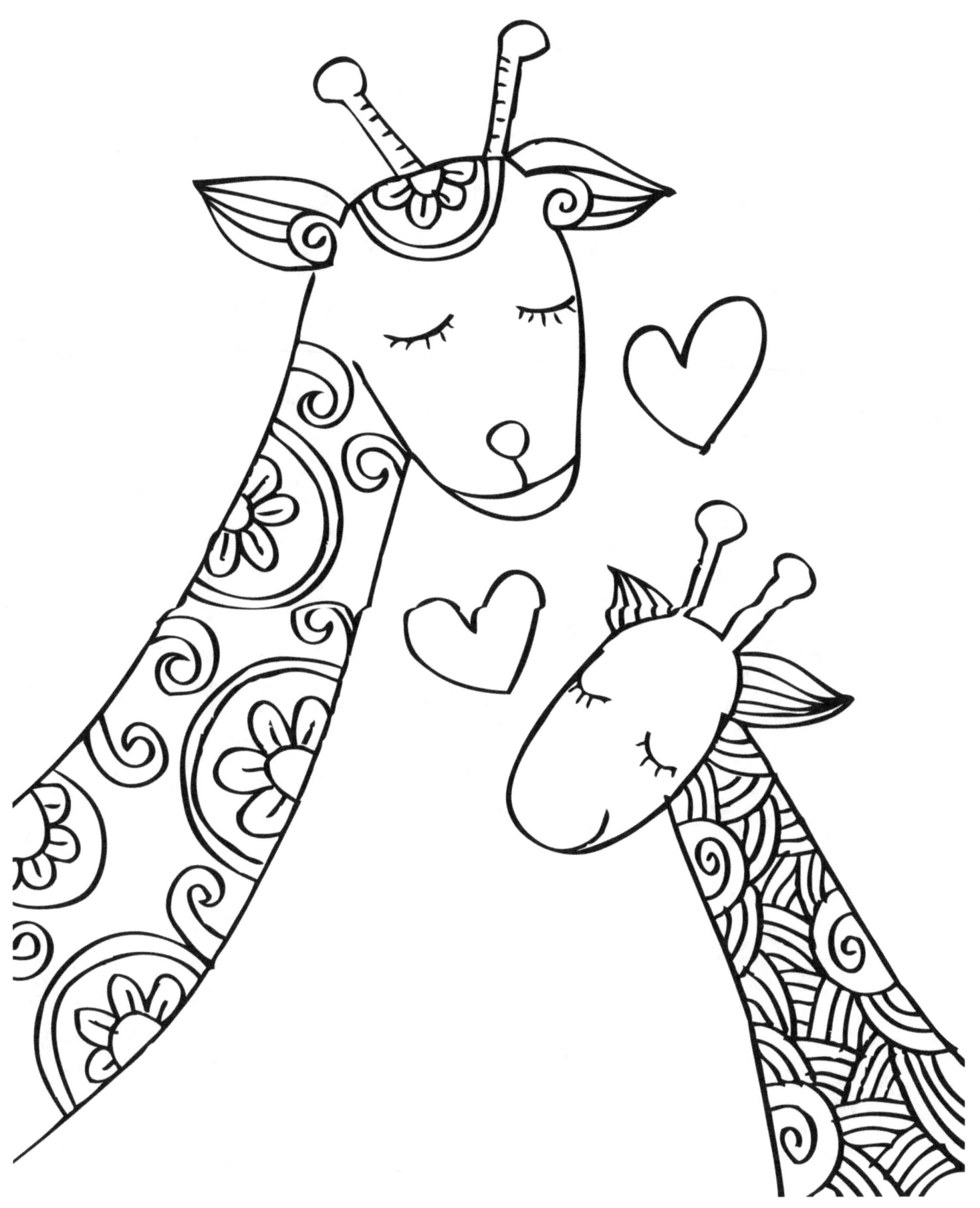

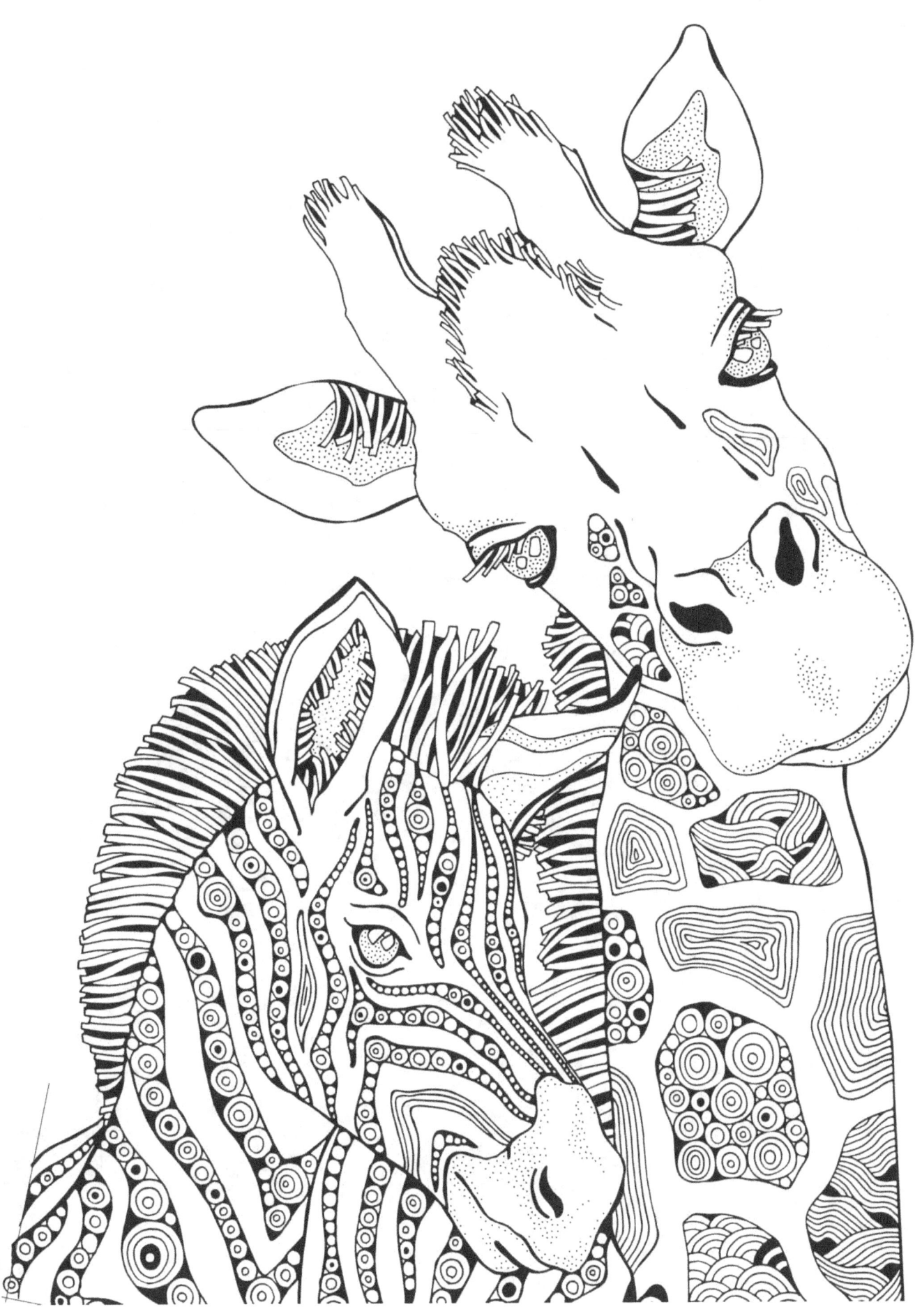

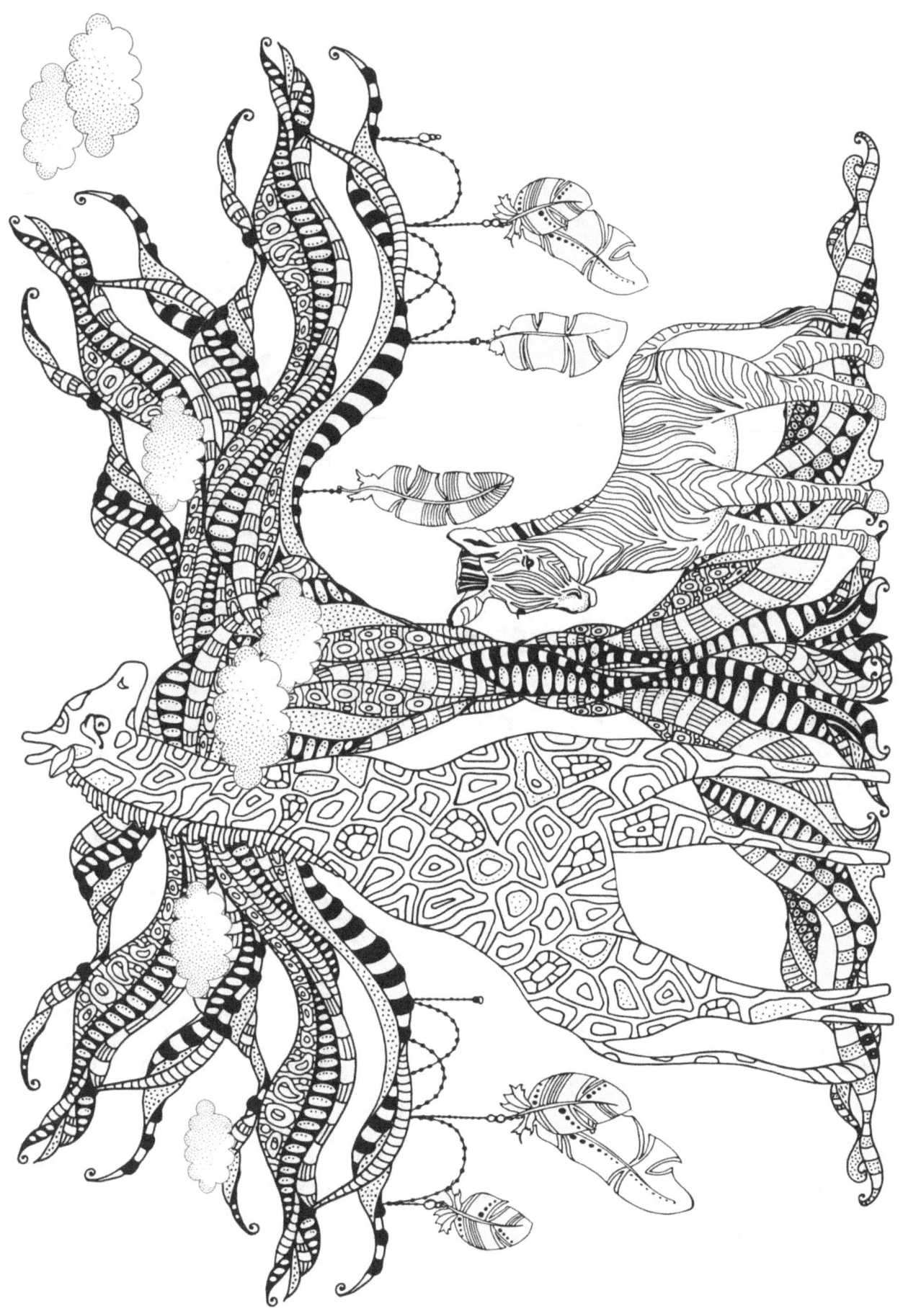

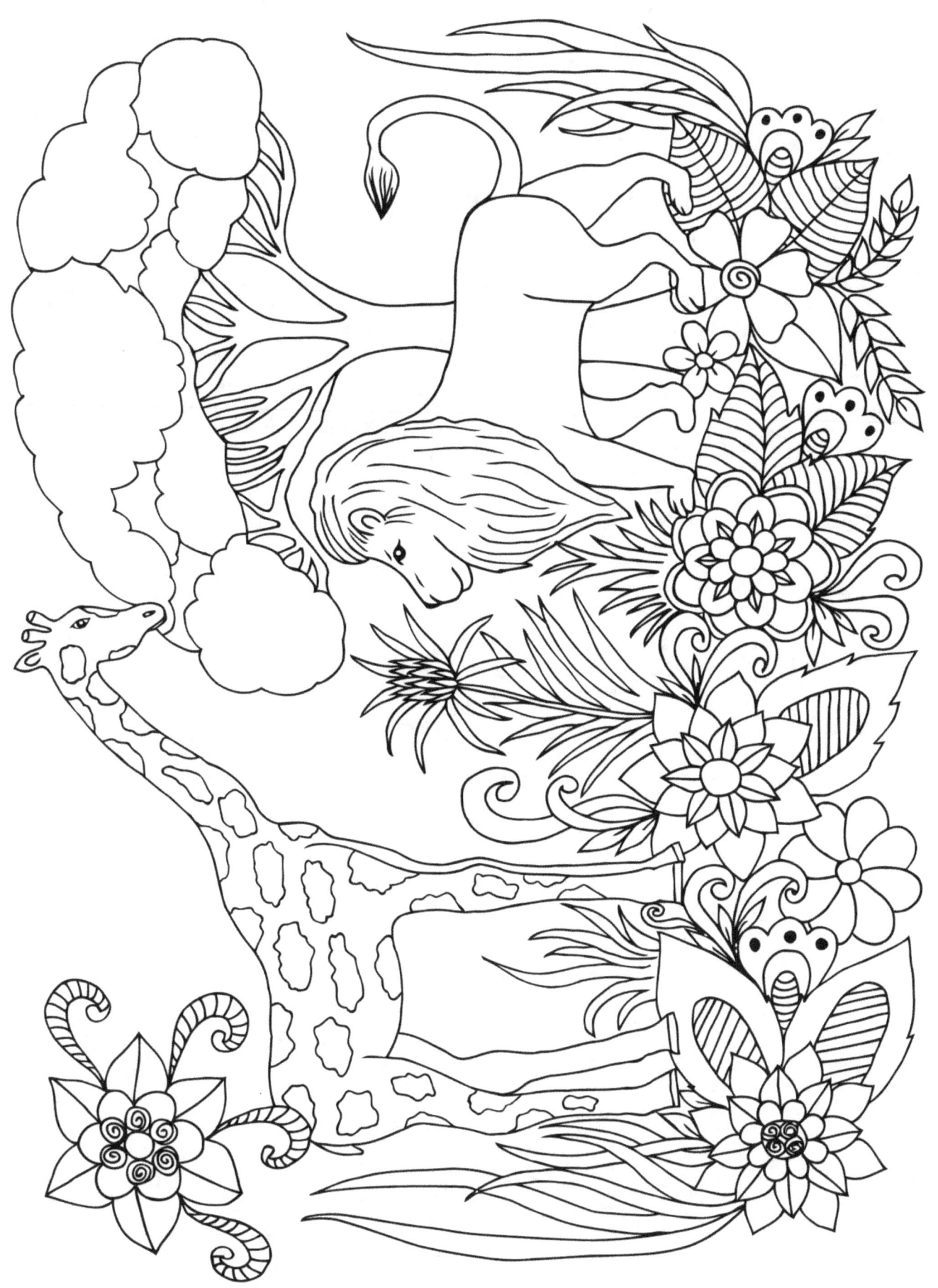

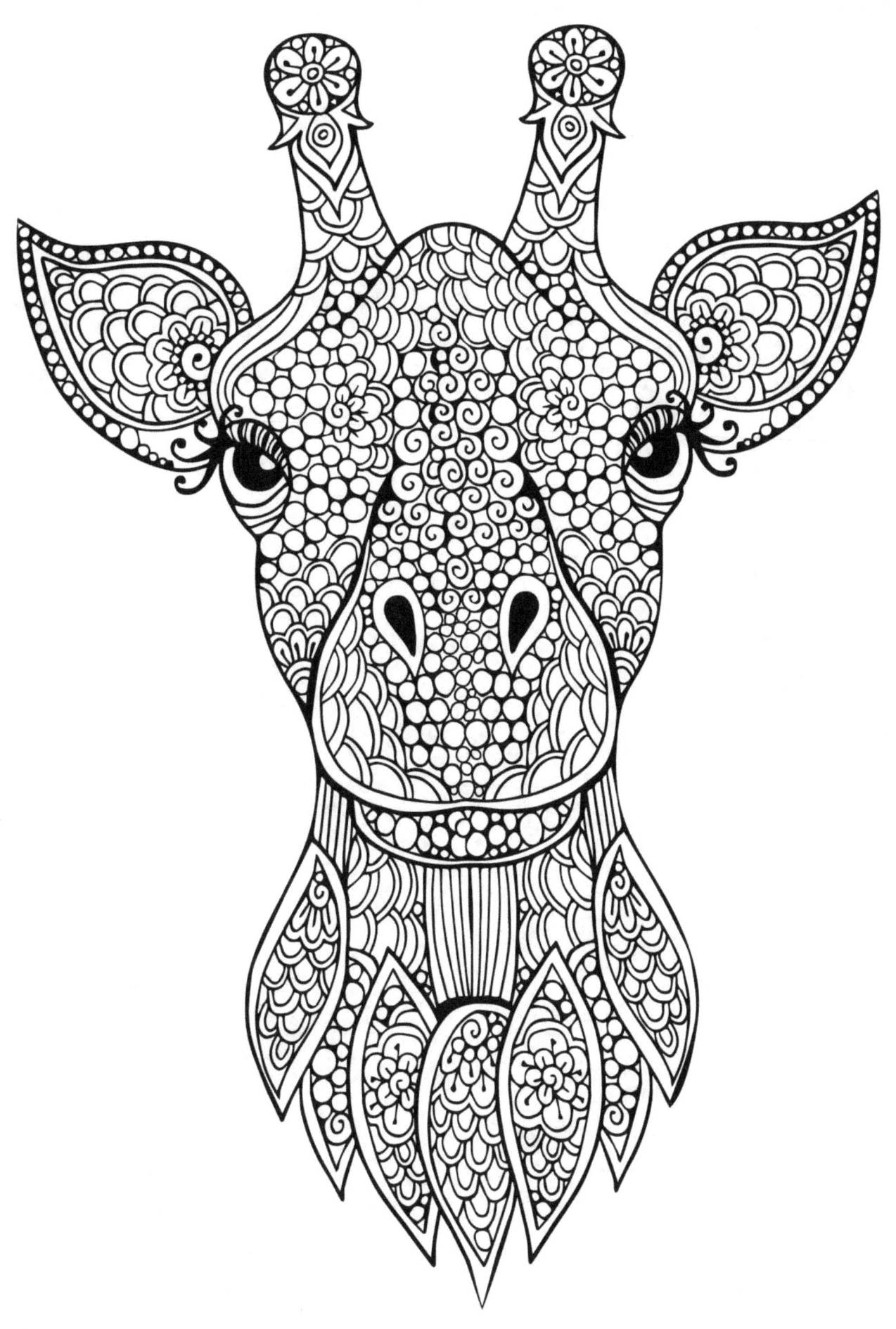

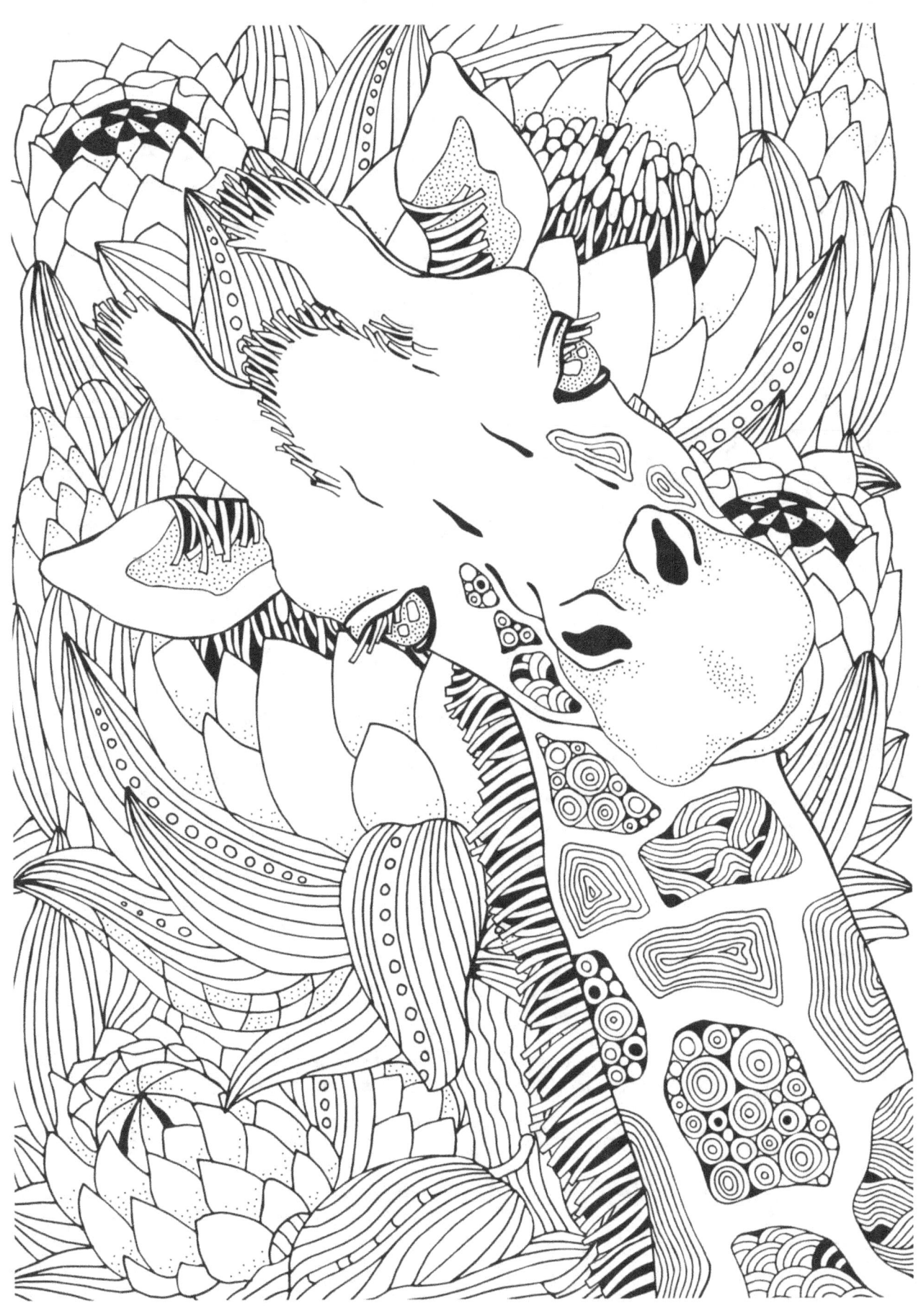

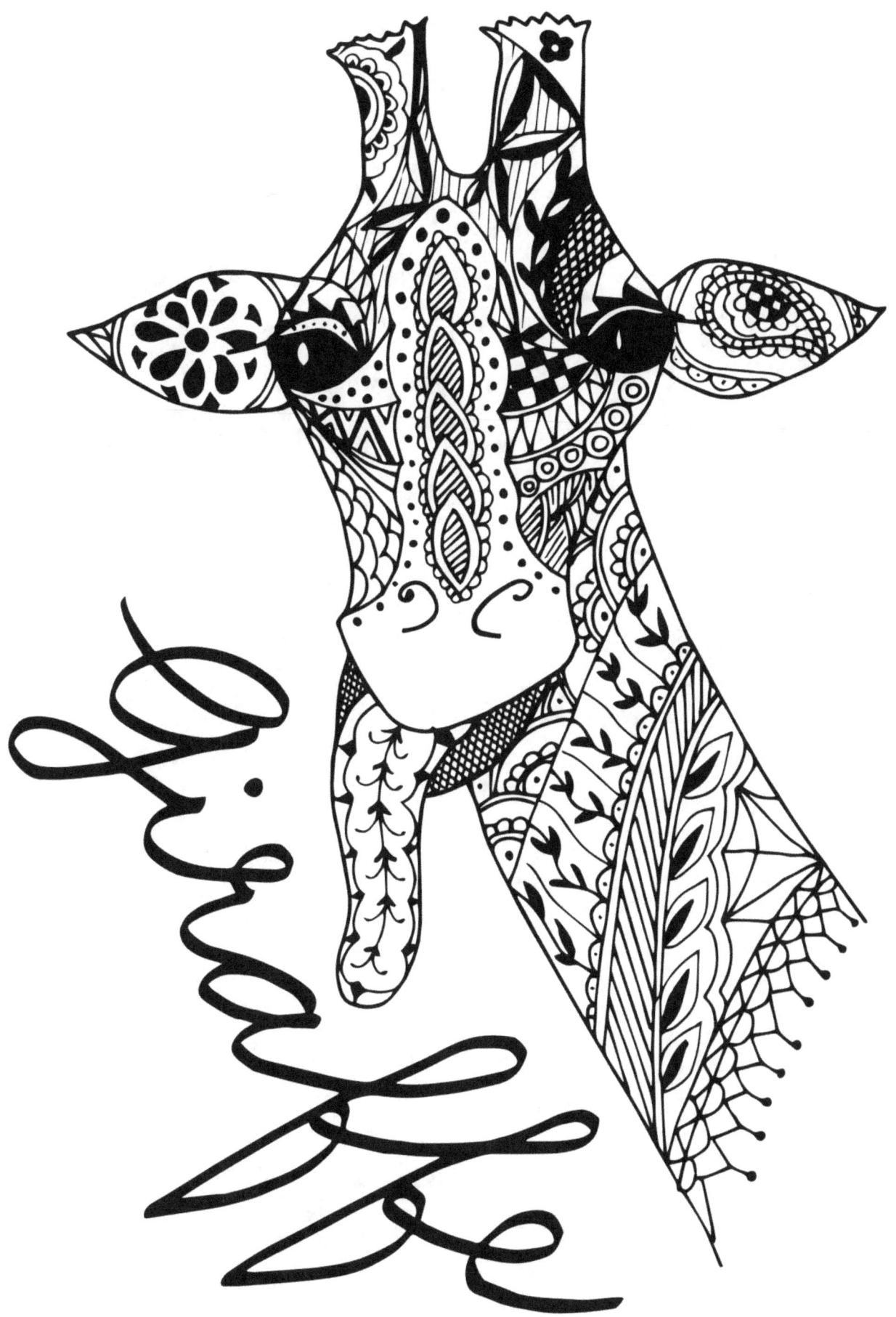

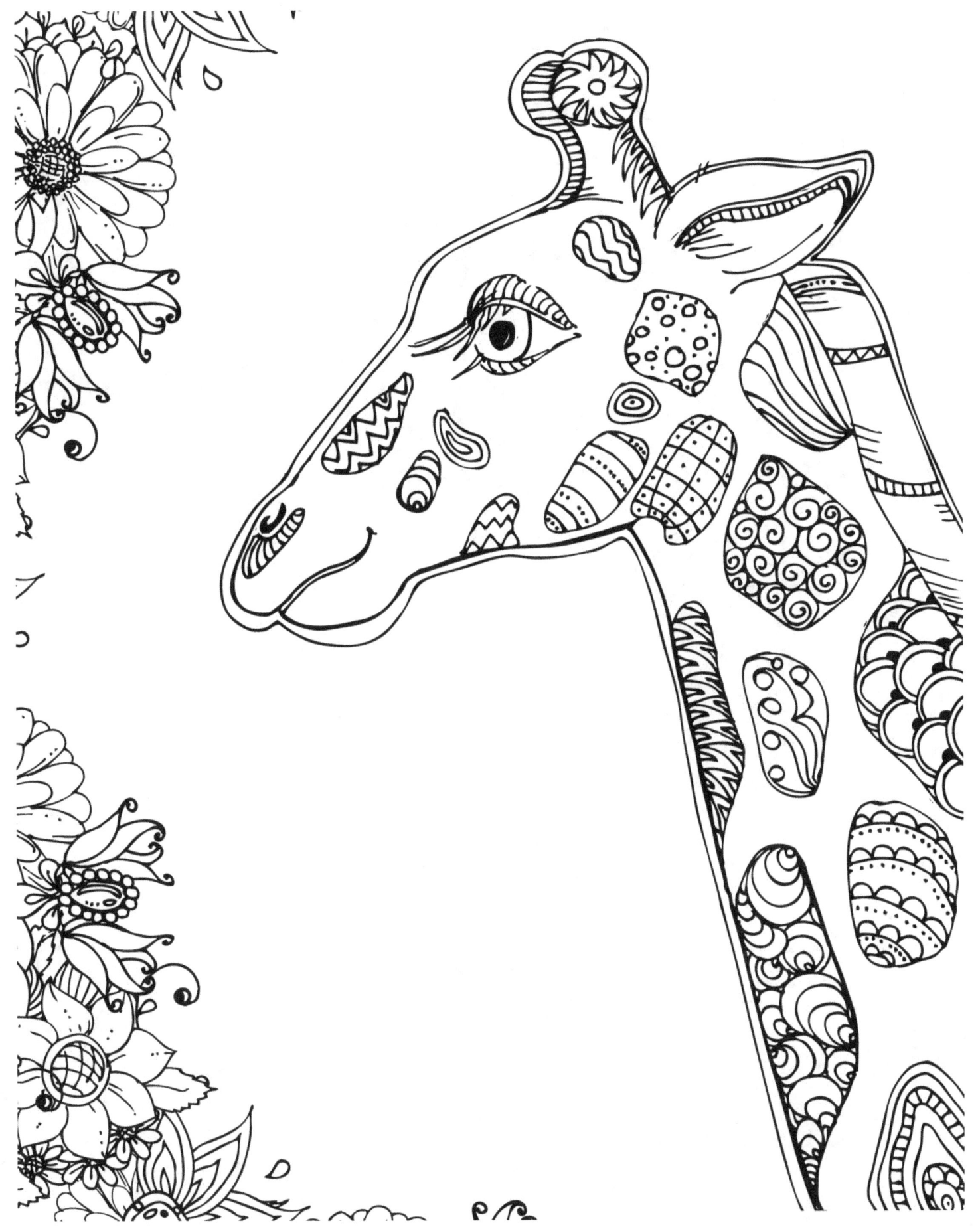

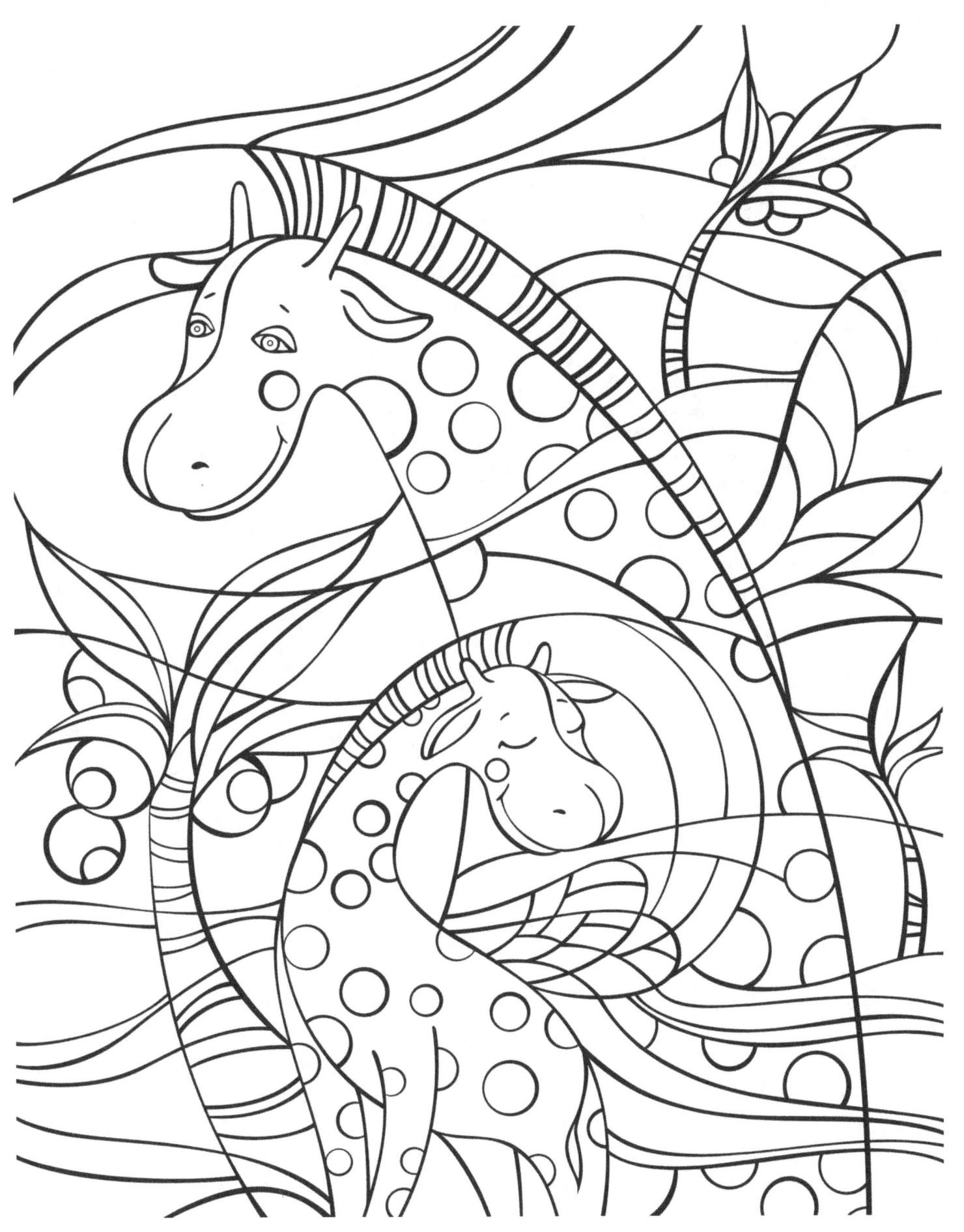

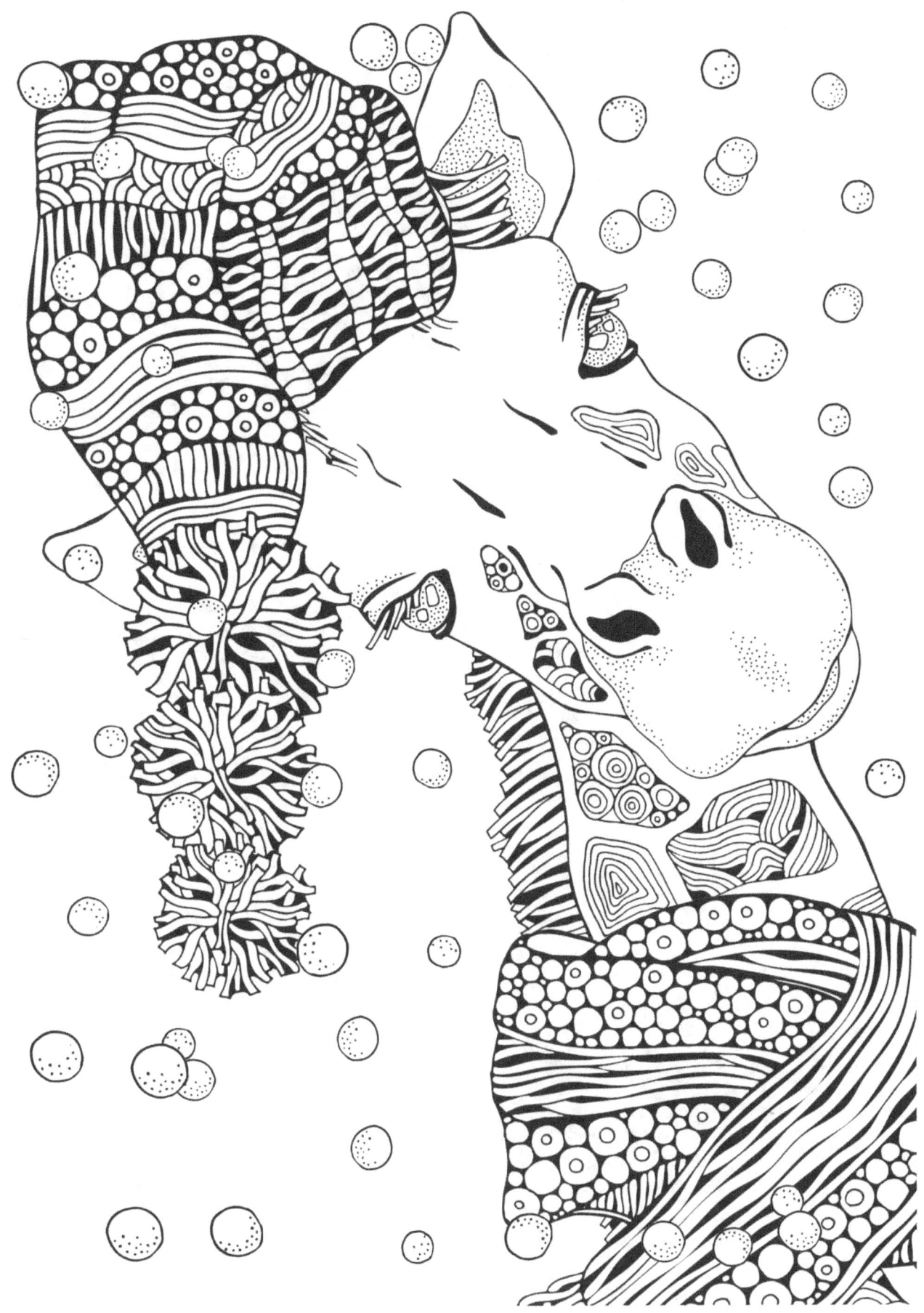

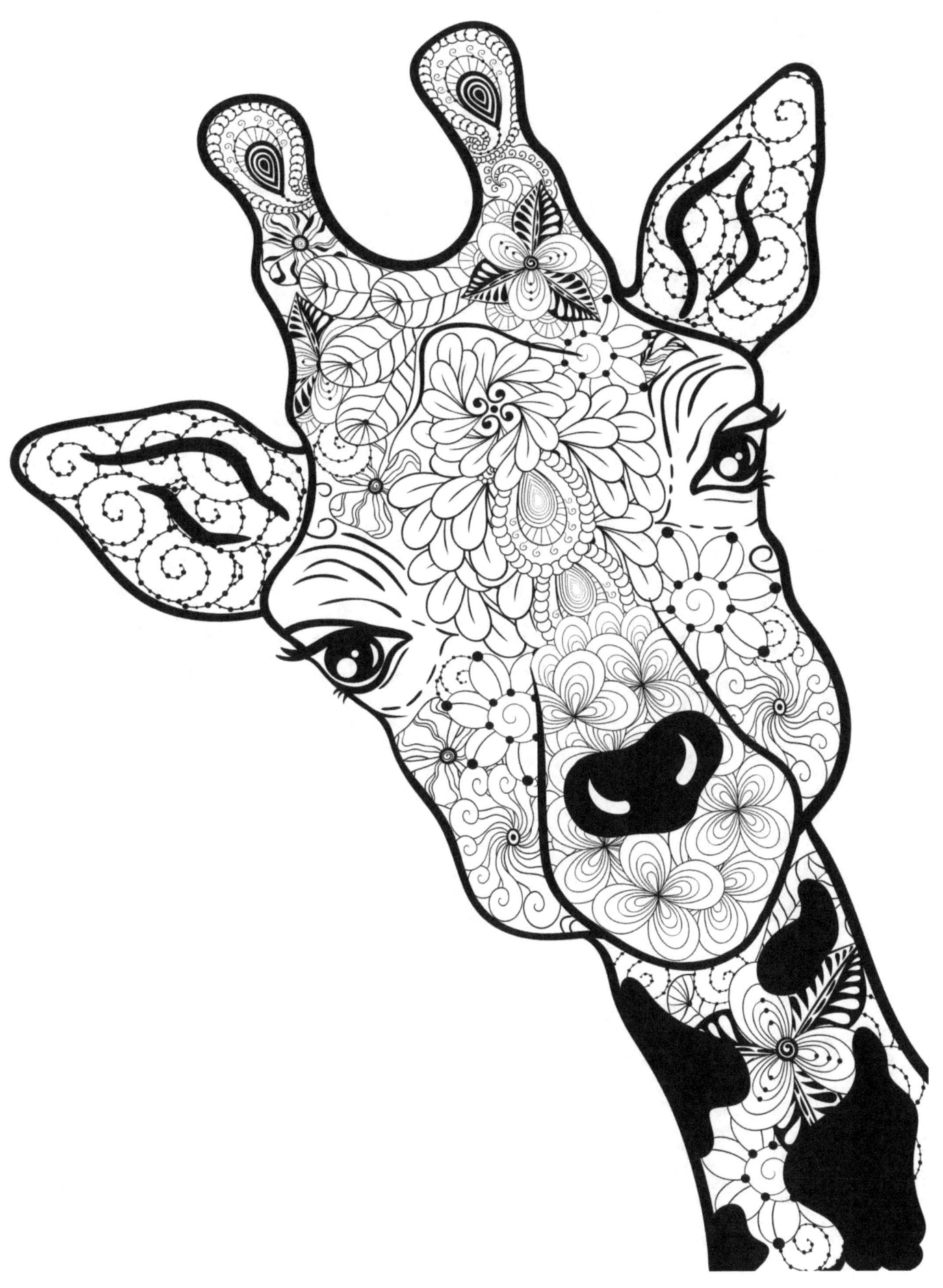

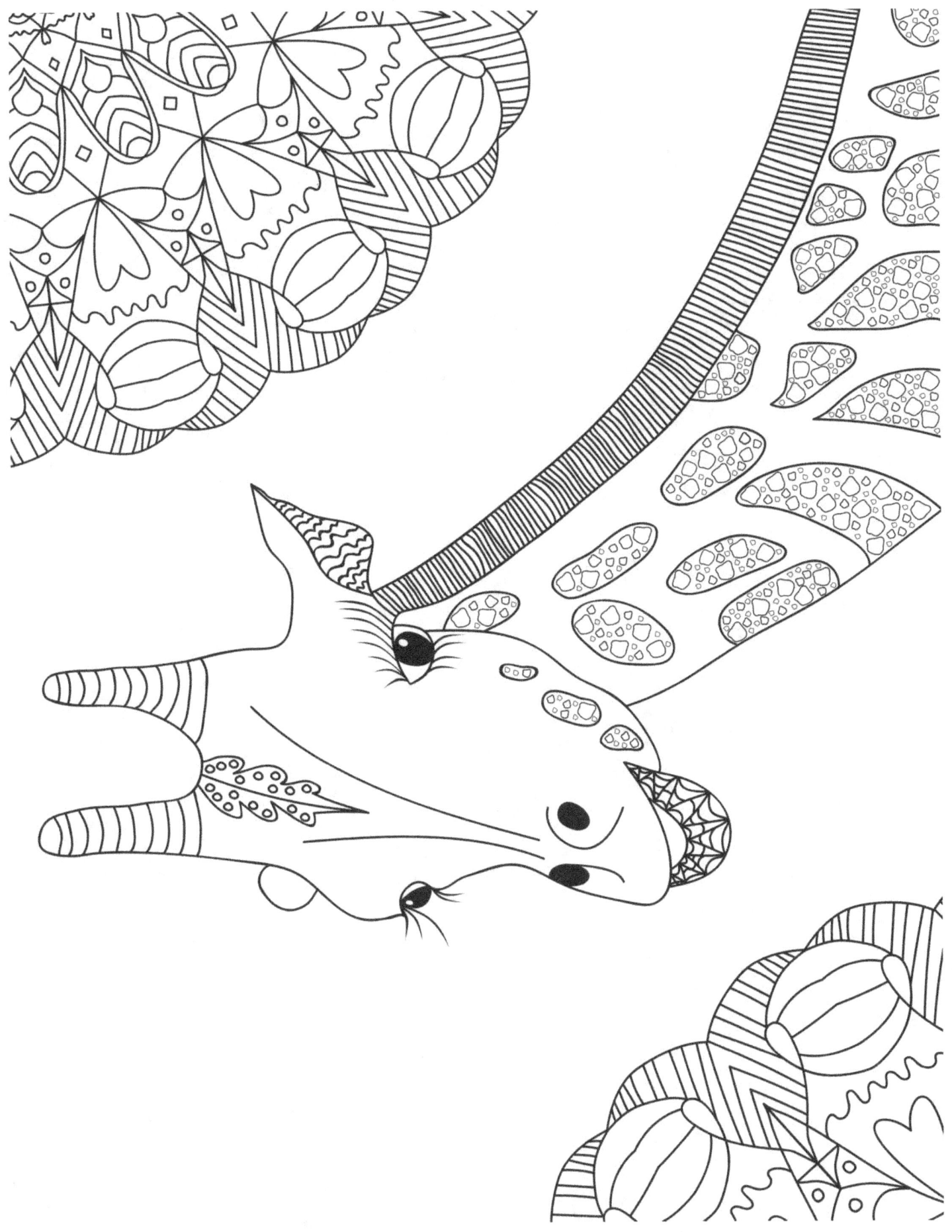

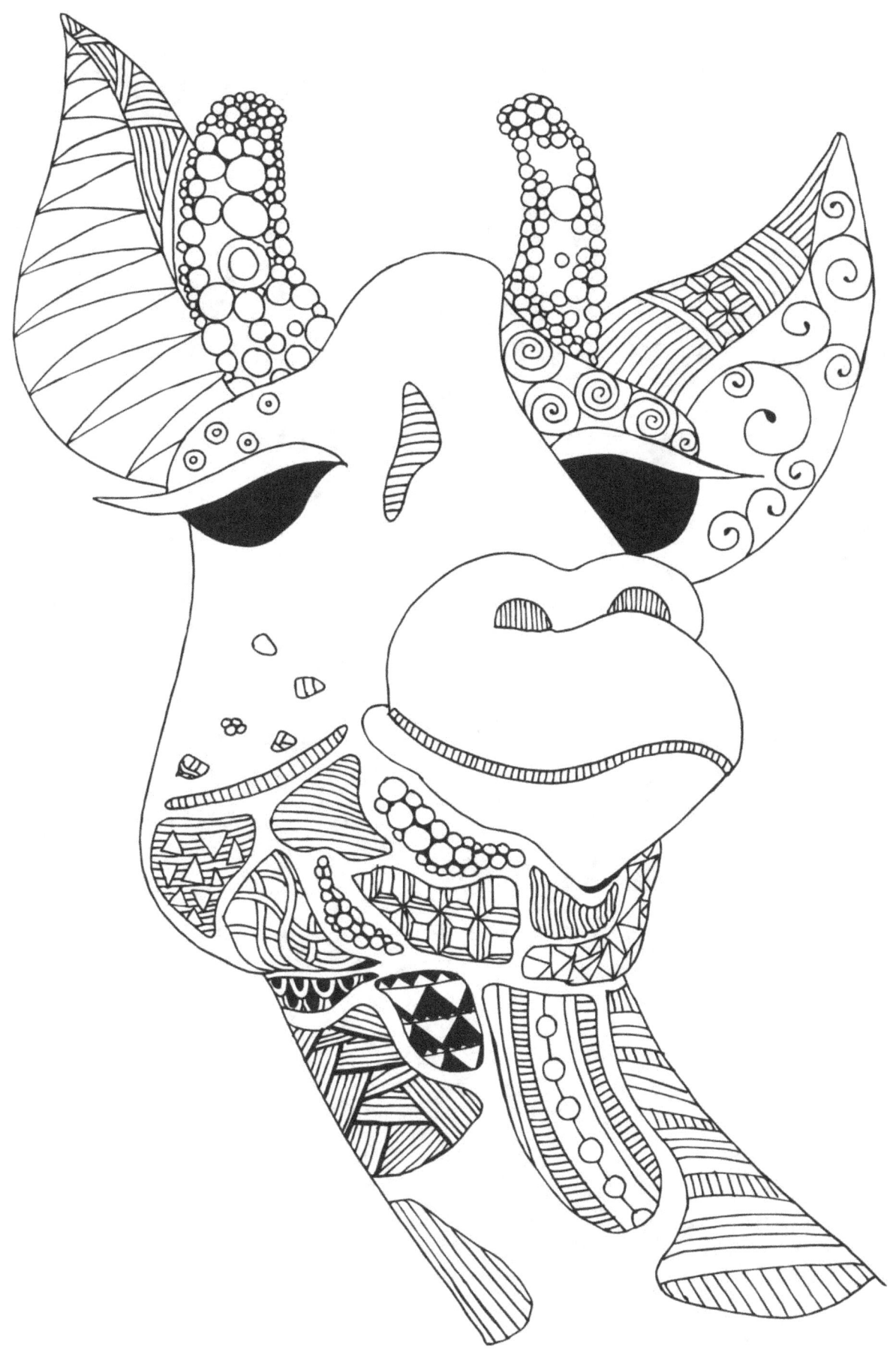

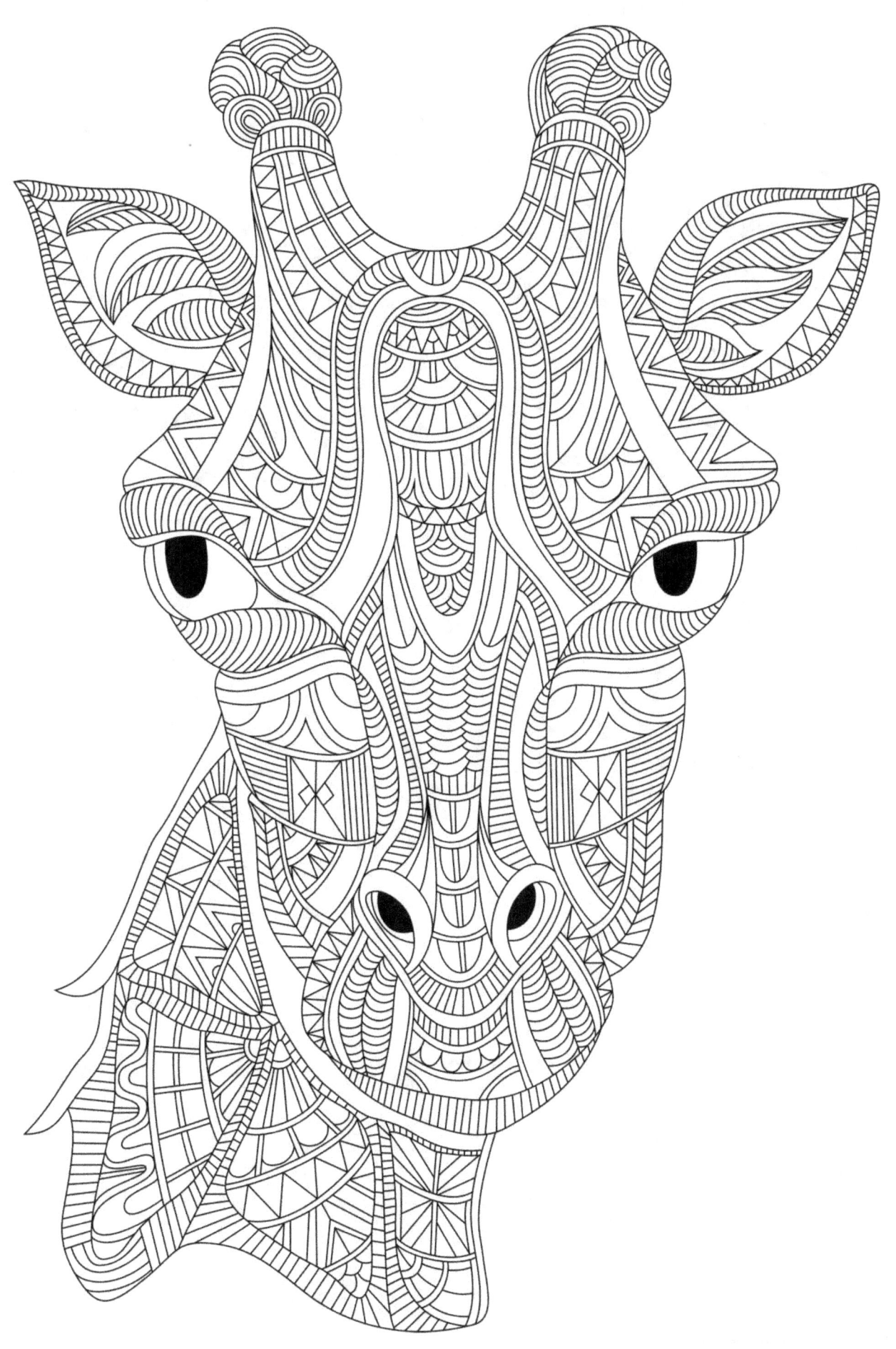

www.ingramcontent.com/pod-product-compliance
Lightning Source LLC
Chambersburg PA
CBHW081250180526
45170CB00007B/2362